The
2-Year-Old's
Guide to
WORK-LIFE
BALANCE

PAUL ARTALE

To Alessio and Sofia for helping me rediscover joy.

To Sherri for loving me and my dreams.

The

2-Year-Old's

Guide

To

WORK-LIFE

Balance

TABLE OF CONTENTS

PROLOGUE

Who is your Yoda? Not a Star Wars fan? Let me rephrase then: who is your Dumbledore, your Olivia Pope from *Scandal*, your Charles S. Dutton in the movie *Rudy* or your Mr. Miyagi from *The Karate Kid?* Maybe you believe that these types of mentors don't exist in real life or perhaps you found wisdom and guidance from a family member, boss, or close friend.

I have been lucky enough to glean wisdom in several arenas of my life in terms of my job, managing my finances, buying a house, etc. I have Yoda's in so many areas except for one: work-life balance.

It's ironic when you learn that the subject of my dissertation research, of my many workshops and keynotes, and my overall passion lies in the realm of work-life balance. I can tell you a lot about it. I can help you find your work-life preference, give you suggestions on defining boundaries, provide worksheets on goal attainment, and even take you through some time management exercises. Need a new career? I can help with that through individualized career coaching. By the way, many of these tools are also going to be available to you because you are awesome and bought this book. I can do all that, but there was a time when I struggled to define it for myself. I wanted a work-life mentor, but the closest I came were through a few books and YouTube videos.

Then in the course of one-week, a larger than life, blond haired, 3'4" cherub with a quick wit and infectious laugh changed my perspective with nine simple phrases. On some levels, I am sure my son Alessio (Ah-Less-Eee-O) was just trying to get me to play with him or agree to give him another cookie. Actually, I *am* pretty darn sure that's what he wanted. Nevertheless, I owe my perspective (and my newfound life) to him.

I was in a weird place emotionally at the time. That's probably why his nine phrases cut through me, and led me to reflect on some deep questions and assumptions about who I am and what I want my life to look like.

Over the next nine chapters, I will show you what a two-year-old taught me about work-life balance. The concepts are simple, but there is a deep complexity that can be learned from the simple things in life. Before we move forward, I want to let you know about two cool bonuses that come with this book:

Activity Book

I have intentionally put reflection questions and an activity section at the back of this book. Work-life balance is a skillset that can only be improved with practice and reflection. That being said, I want you to enjoy the story and do not want to interrupt the flow of the book. Feel free to flip to the back after every chapter or glance at them when you are done with the story. Finally, if you hate writing in books then you can find a fillable .pdf version of the activity book by going to this site:

www.paulartale.com/2yearoldsguide

Book Bonuses

This book is not just a book. By purchasing *The 2-Year-Old's Guide to Work-Life Balance* you will also receive the following bonus items:

- "Setting Your Work-Life Boundaries" mini e-course.
- *Leaving Your Job* podcast and worksheet.

- *Access to my work-life article, blog, and podcast archive*

These resources are also available by visiting:

www.paulartale.com/2yearoldsguide

Let's Start The Story...

My story begins with all the stress and preparation that comes with leaving town on a business trip brings. I left for Nashville excited to see some honkey tonks and the Johnny Cash Museum. I couldn't imagine it would be the catalyst for a life changing experience. Here is what happened . . .

CHAPTER 1: WHY?

I stormed through the house wildly that night, trying to find the right attire for the future vice-presidents (FVP) conference. I had been looking forward to this conference (and the host city of Nashville, Tennessee) for months. This conference was to help prepare mid-level managers on their path to becoming vice-presidents. In my mind, becoming a vice president was going to give me the professional and financial freedom that I craved. The upward path was the path to a better life in every way.

A third of my clothes were in the dryer, a third in the washer, and the other third smashed into my suitcase. Alessio watched me in amusement as I grunted and stomped through my bedroom. The dryer let out an irritating buzz. I snatched the next set of clothes and leaped towards my luggage.

"Daddy pack bag?" Alessio asked. In full disclosure, he probably asked three or four times before I muttered some form of "yes" back in his general direction.

"Why?"

I stopped for a moment to humor him. "Daddy is going to a conference for work."

"Why?"

"Because Daddy is going to learn how to be better at his work."

"Why?"

"Because Daddy wants to do more important things with his work."

4

"Why?"

"So Daddy can make more money and pay for nice things for Alessio and Mommy."

Silence. I had won . . . for about ten seconds. I started to fold my beloved Superman t-shirt when he chimed up again.

"Why?"

"Because nice things mean that we can have fun."

"Why?"

I wanted to reply with *"So we don't have to be poor, so you can go to good schools, have great healthcare, and investment options,"* but I don't think he would have understood. I also did not want to introduce the concept of poverty to a two year old, even if he could possibly grasp it. Instead, I answered with:

"Because fun things make Daddy happy."

That answer seemed to satisfy him. Alessio quieted down and continued to watch me pack the rest of the suitcase.

As I packed, I started to reflect on those *why* questions. Why was I doing this? Was the journey to the top really just about money, security, and importance? How happy would it make me beyond that?

Ten years earlier, I had hastily filled my luggage with whatever I deemed useful and moved from Toronto to Kansas with no money and a desire to succeed. I was twenty-four years old and although I had a steady job as a high school history teacher, I had a deep passion for coaching football. I applied to some college coaching jobs (with no intention of being hired) and as luck would have it I was offered a position as an assistant coach at a small college in Kansas. To help pay my bills (coaching college football does not pay much at the small college level) I also took a job overseeing a residence hall at the college because it came with a free apartment. The apartment itself was infested with roaches and horseflies. I told myself, *this is part of paying my dues, right?* Besides, I was able to spend almost every day on a football field and that was incredible to me. It didn't matter that I was poor and starving because I was happy. Nothing else mattered.

The first summer I coached college football saw me live on cheap groceries. My menu consisted of ramen noodles, no name bologna, tuna, fruits from the clearance bin and whatever food I could take from staff meetings and university functions. This became the basis for one of the first inspirational speeches that I gave called *The Treasure.* *The Treasure* would also be a speech that I gave during my first visit to the World Championships of Public Speaking where I was among the final 90 out of over 32,000 contestants. *The Treasure* wasn't just a speech about living as a poor assistant coach. It was about how a terrible car accident that my father was in made me realize the importance of family. Family was so important that I promised myself that I would emerge from this poverty den as soon as possible and never look back.

The years moved on and I climbed the ranks quickly. I eventually gave up coaching football (a decision I was ok with but did not come lightly), became a mid-level manager in university administration and slowly but surely increased my income. In ten short years, I had a house I loved in a great neighborhood and enough expendable income to live a comfortable life. I still ate ramen noodles, but when I did, it was out of some strange sense of nostalgia and it was Top Ramen. A guy has to treat himself, right? Still, I wanted more. I wanted to climb higher. That's why this conference was important. It would show me some useful next steps on my journey.

The journey began at four a.m. as I battled a frosty Michigan morning to get to the airport. The good thing about early morning flights is that the airport is usually dead and you can get through security quickly. I found myself with more than an hour to spare as I tried to stay awake at the gate. It was there that I met Hugo. Hugo was a doctor with thick glasses, grey stubble and a very welcoming smile. He reminded me of the legendary playwright Neil Simon.

As we made small talk, Hugo asked me where I was going and why. I told him I was going to an aspiring vice-presidents conference. I mentioned that it would be nice to be making a six-figure salary one day relatively soon.

Hugo immediately fired back with, "Why not a seven figure salary?"

I chuckled. "Not in my business. But I do speaking and consulting on the side. That can take me to seven figures one day and it's fun!"

"Tell me more about the speaking," he said.

I proceeded to tell him about my story of overcoming physical disability to play and coach college football, my love for leadership development training, and how I didn't do nearly enough training or speaking in my current job. I wished I could do more of that on a daily basis instead of creating and enforcing campus policies or helping students decide what the catering should be for the all-campus formal.

Hugo gave me a satisfied look before replying, "Well, maybe you should put more of your efforts there."

"So I can make seven figures?"

Hugo shook his head. "No, because it's fun and I can see on your face that you love it."

"Yeah . . ." I took a long pause. "Speaking is one of the few places where life makes sense to me."

"Do what fulfills you. You will find the money you need and you will be happy. And a happy person is usually a healthy person. Take my word on that one."

I definitely was not going to argue with him on that last point . . . or any of those points. I asked myself "why" again . . . this time about being a speaker and leadership trainer. Alessio's voice rang in my head. *Why?* Why did I want to do it?

"Because speaking is fun and makes me happy."

"Why?"

"Because I get to be creative and free from so many of the restrictions in my work-life."

"Why?"

"Because that freedom leads to me spreading my message so that I can help people become successful or overcome challenges."

"Why?"

"Because some people need help and need some advice, or just to hear that someone with similar experiences succeeded."

"Why?"

"Because helping people is fun and makes me happy. It is fulfilling."

There it was. From that point on it was hard to justify my current path. Anything else seemed like an excuse or bartering happiness for money. The chorus of *whys* uncovered a truth in me that was now hard to ignore. Don't get me wrong. I tried to ignore them. I hadn't even started my conference after all.

** The Lesson **

Like so many people, I was raised to buy into the traditional and linear process of work and life. You know the one. It goes something like this:

1)   Go to school.
2)   Get a good job that has good salary and benefits.
3)   Start a family (you may swap points 2 and 3 if you want)
4)   Die.

It is a system that implies very specific checkpoints and standards. It puts the reward on doing the "safe" thing. We are encouraged to pick an occupation and stick with it. Doing what we love for a living is great, but it is not necessary. The people that manage to follow their passions, make a good living, and enjoy their work-life are presented as mythical heroes. They are the exception, not the rule. We are sold the *do what you love* story until we graduate school and are told to get a job. At that point, most dreams and passions get relegated to hobby status. But it's ok, right? We'll have a good career and eventually we will find fulfillment or carve out the time to dabble in a passion project or two. All will be well. It's the classic square peg in round hole scenario. It's like when I was a kid and you had the real LEGO and the softer, slightly larger imitation LEGO. On the surface, they looked the same, but you couldn't get the two to properly fit.

Why do you do what you do? Why is it important? The ingrained response might be: I do it to get a job and it is important because I need to pay bills. That just doesn't cut it for most people in the long term. Of course, we all have basic needs that need to get met, but once we obtain a position that meets those needs, the joy of working quickly loses its appeal. We begin to want more and/or tolerate imbalances between work and life far less. If our *why* was rooted in just paying bills and making a living, then I'm certain more people would be reporting greater satisfaction at work. It may also result in less stress and anxiety health-wise. For most of us, there is a bigger *why* buried deep that wants to come out.

Another problem with our ingrained notions of work and life is that it tries to funnel us into a way of life that is safe, comfortable. It also avoids one of the most important questions that is crucial to developing our work-life balance: *what's the why? Why* do you do what you do?

Simon Sinek is a popular author, motivational speaker, and organizational consultant who wrote the book *Start With Why*. Sinek is famous for challenging us to *start with why* as a mode of leadership and entrepreneurship. On the topic of values and principles Sinek writes:

"It's not 'integrity,' it's 'always do the right thing.' It's not 'innovation,' it's 'look at the problem from a different angle.'"

Your work-life journey has to start with *why* as well. It requires you to look at your situation from a different angle. It asks that you live the values and beliefs you claim. *Why* are you living the life you are right now? *Why* are you doing the work you do? *Why* don't you change things that bother you? *Why* are you holding on to assumptions that are keeping you from living the life you want? *Why* are you delaying taking steps to improve your work, your life, and all the domains in between?

What's *your* why?

Deep down, I think you know what it is. If you don't, then you need to turn off the technology, shut the door and do some serious reflecting. Even when we can *feel* our why we cannot always *express* our why.

This may seem very idealistic and rhetorical, but drilling down with *why* is where you have to start if you want to bring some peace between your work and your personal life. If there is balance and harmony, great! If there isn't then ask *why*. *Why* isn't there harmony and peace? When you have those answers then you can find ways to make that harmony a reality. If you can't, then ask *why* again.

What's your why? is the first and most important question for you to answer. What would that job look like, and what about it would make you jump out of bed and say "I can't wait to get to work today?" What type of work and lifestyle would excite you? What would make you approach every day with an unstoppable energy to take on the world. What would make you work into the wee hours of the night without noticing it?

To look at it another way, the question is trying to assess if your life is purpose driven. My purpose has always been to educate, and, more specifically, to educate people on how to live their best lives. Ask yourself, if money wasn't an issue, what type of work would you select and why? What are the elements that would make that possible, and how does that compare to your current situation? For example, one of the key elements that I enjoy as a speaker is schedule control. Schedule control is exactly what it sounds like – the ability for a person to control their schedule. My situation at the time had almost no schedule control, and it was causing me strain.

WHAT'S YOUR WHY?

Tweet me @PaulArtale and tell me. Use #2yearoldsguide

CHAPTER 2: SO HAPPY

Nashville was fun. I visited some honky tonks, learned more about Johnny Cash than I ever imagined, and had a great time walking around exploring the city. Sadly, a stomach bug was keeping me from tasting a lot of good ol' southern cooking. Luckily, I met some great colleagues at the conference who took my mind off food (or the lack of it in my system at the time).

As a child, I always wanted my mother when I was sick. As a father, I really just wanted to hang with my son who can make me chuckle and smile in any circumstance. I set up a Skype meeting the first morning of the conference. I could hear Alessio's babble through a black screen. He sounded happy and playful even if he didn't seem to be speaking English at that exact moment. A few seconds later his image came through the camera.

There was his face, sideways, and shooting me his car salesman-like smile. A devilish giggle soon followed. I attempted to make small talk with him, but he just kept staring and smiling. I could hear my wife, Sherri, in the background trying to coax some conversation out of him to no avail. Eventually Alessio resumed running around the house, and flinging toys across the room. It was business as usual.

I took the opportunity to talk to Sherri to see how she and our baby (she was five months pregnant at the time) were doing. Eventually the conversation turned to me, the conference, and my constant obsession with planning the next twenty years of my life.

Sensing my wife's boredom, Alessio interrupted me.

14

"DADDY!"

Finally! I had been acknowledged.

"Are you happy?"

. . . not quite what I was expecting. "Yeah, buddy, I am happy."

"Daddy, SO happy?"

Man, this kid is relentless. "Yes, Alessio. Daddy is SO happy."

His enormous on-screen figure suddenly disappeared, and from the sounds of it, started chasing the cat. I have to admit, I felt a little guilty. I had lied to my son because I never actually really thought about what he was asking. I was just trying to get him to move on to another phrase or conversation topic.

Was I happy? Yes. Although my *why,* the passion that motivates me may not have been entirely in my job, I was happy. In many ways, I liked my job. I was content on most days. Alessio, however, wasn't asking me if I was happy or content. He was asking if I was SO happy. Like a good PhD student, I analyzed.

Have you ever been thirsty? Perhaps a tad parched? When you are very thirsty, you're likely go look for something to drink that meets your needs, right?

Have you ever been SO thirsty? The type of thirst you might get after a workout or on a hot day, or just by going way too long without a beverage. You are SO thirsty. You rush into the house, fling open the refrigerator and guzzle the first thing that you see. For instance, there was the time that I mistook pickle juice for apple juice. I was SO thirsty I didn't think about it, or in my case, remember I had poured the pickle juice into a smaller apple juice container to save refrigerator space.

The word SO was throwing me for a loop. What did SO happy mean anyway? I can remember the first time I put on the blue and white football jersey of the University of Toronto. It represented a dream that came to fruition. For someone who was born with a physical challenge, it also symbolized triumph over adversity. That day I was SO happy. Five years later, I would marry my wife Sherri in front of all my friends and family. She was beautiful, the day was perfect, and the party rocked! I was definitely SO happy that day. However, at the moment Alessio asked me . . . well . . . I wasn't SO sure.

I was happy, but I wasn't SO happy. I wasn't busting with joy and so happy that if something went wrong, I would remain unaffected. I wasn't SO happy that people who ran into me would say, "Wow, you're one happy dude!" Instead, I was hearing a lot of, "Are you doing better today?" or "What's wrong?" I will admit, my default facial expression is a cross between deep thought and constant annoyance, but lately, nobody was mistaking me for being happy, let alone SO Happy.

** The Lesson **

The word *so* is the key here. You can replace *so* with words like *extremely* or *tremendously* or any other synonym. It's about experiencing a form of happiness that is enduring and immediately recognizable to you. If somebody asks if you are happy (let alone SO happy) you should be able to answer "yes" right away. Sure, we have all have bad days or

16

weeks. However, if the happiness is enduring, then we know the pain is only temporary. To better understand *so happy*, I want to discuss three concepts that funnel into it: satisfaction, life giving, and resilience.

Satisfaction

I have seen many nuanced definitions of satisfaction. In many respects, the definition satisfaction is based on the context in which we use it. Job satisfaction is different than life satisfaction, which will differ from satisfaction with your health. The word satisfaction itself is Latin in origin, coming from the past participle of the word *satisfacere*. *Satis* meaning enough and *facere* meaning to make, or do).

Thusly, satisfaction at its root means to make enough (or to do enough). I like the former definition because *making enough* is more dynamic, and in line with the philosophy of this book. We may know what *enough* is, but we may not be currently in a position that allows for that to happen. A simple example is living in that small starter home or apartment. We know that one day we want to own a bigger home/condo, but our current reality will not allow it. Thus we can save, work extra jobs, and sell items we don't need any more etc., in order to make this a reality. We are *making enough.*

Some of you may be thinking "Well, isn't wanting bigger and better one of the major factors that lead to dissatisfaction?" To that, I'll say two things. One: don't confuse *making enough* (aka satisfaction) with wanting more. Two: To avoid the confusion of point one, you have to know what *enough* is. It is something that we all have to define for ourselves. This concept was discussed at length at the conference in Nashville when we spoke about the salaries of vice presidents. I remember a very seasoned and respected vice president at university saying, "You have to decide what an acceptable salary range and lifestyle is for you, because it varies in this business. Know what you need versus falling in love with a mythical number." It was great advice.

The marketing genius Alan Weiss who is famous for the book *Million Dollar Consulting* frames this concept of enough in a way that is less theoretical and more to the point. In one of his keynotes to a group of aspiring speakers, Alan tells the story of how he was in Monaco, and saw a yacht with three swimming pools on it. The yacht was worth $30 million and Alan could care less. Although Alan himself was wealthy, he knew what enough was for him, and didn't fall into the trap of wanting more.

Satisfaction, however, goes beyond money, houses, and yachts. If we go back to the dictionary (and skip the Latin lesson), we see it is defined as an act of *fulfilment* or *gratification.* As an aside, *satisfaction* can also be defined as the opportunity to redress or right a wrong, as by a duel. That can be relevant if we look at challenging our current assumptions about what we truly need to be happy. Satisfaction, then, is about what fulfills us. And for the record, there will be no pistols at dawn in this book. Perhaps in the sequel. I haven't decided yet.

The term *job satisfaction* deals with how much fulfilment we get from our job (duh). There has been a lot of research done on job satisfaction, and, in a nutshell, here is what has been found. Salary is not as big a determinant of satisfaction as you would think. People need enough money to be comfortable, but what drives them away from a job often has less to do with compensation and benefits, and more to do with professional development, growth opportunities, and workplace relationships (especially with management). Let me explain that a different way. Money isn't what satisfies people nearly as much as the chance to fulfill their professional desires. Being treated respectfully and having a sense of belonging to an organization do more for an employee's satisfaction than a mere paycheck.

When you aren't respected at work or when the work doesn't excite or push you to be better, then you have a higher likelihood of being dissatisfied. Being dissatisfied at work increases your chances of being dissatisfied with other parts of your life as well. This is often referred to as *spillover*. *Spillover* can be positive, though. You can be energized and invigorated at work, and have that carry over to how you interact with your family. Conversely, you can be miserable in your work, and come home and take *that* out on your family. When this happens to me, Sherri calls me a 'snappy turtle'. If we want to go even deeper, *spillover* can seep from your personal life into your working environment, as well. I remember going into work the Monday after I won a karate tournament. I was great to be around the office that day. Contrast that with when Alessio was in the hospital with pneumonia when he was six months old, and it's safe to say I wasn't at my most pleasant or effective. It's all interrelated. Work affects our happiness at home, and home affects our happiness at work. Given that most of us spend most of our time working, paying attention to how our jobs impact our satisfaction has to be given greater attention.

So let's tie some of this together with a quick *satisfaction* quiz. Please note it has been analyzed, weighted, tested, and has a Cronbach Alpha score of .93 (which is a fancy way of saying it measures what it says it will measure). Ready? Here it is.

Are you satisfied with your job?   [   ] Yes   [   ] No

Ok, seriously, go to the activity section for this chapter to take a quick satisfaction assessment.

Life Giving

I had the honor of working with a priest by the name of Father Graham. I was working as a residence hall director at a small university when we first met. The job was similar to being a landlord or property manager except the tenants all knew where you lived, and both students and administration had no problems accessing you 24-7. The climate of the environment I was in was toxic, and I was considering shaking things up and moving on to another institution. I was miserable in my job, and wanted a change of some sort. I struggled to define that change. Before I would ramble too much about work and jobs, Father Graham would always lightly interject with his calm, soothing voice:

"Well if you aren't doing things that are *life-giving*, then why do them?"

For the longest time, my only answers were "I need the money" or "This is the career path I am on. I have to stick it out." Father Graham would shake his head negatively. He said nothing. It was his way of telling me to keep digging for an answer. Finally, one day I exclaimed, "This place isn't right for me. A continued career in residence hall management is not right for me. My change needs to be away from here and this line of work. I have no valid *why* right now. I want to educate leaders and spread my message. That's what is *life giving*. That's what I need to do."

Silence . . . then a smirk. Followed by: "You are thinking right."

20

So what does *life-giving* mean? *Life-giving* means to engage in activities and endeavors that sustain, grow, and fulfill us. *Life-giving* activities have the ability to give us power and spirit. *Life giving* exists and thrives in a lifestyle that makes you feel alive and bustling with energy (aka *so happy*) versus just happy and there (aka happy) or in some cases just flat out unhappy or miserable. Finally, *life-giving* activities not only grow you personally, but they benefit and empower those around you, as well.

Let us look at *life giving* in action. My friend Chalis Sledge Henderson started a scholarship many years ago. She wanted to create a mechanism by which members of her former high school, and her community at large could benefit from. She poured her effort into this, and the scholarship grew from awarding a single $250 scholarship to one recipient to two $5,000 scholarships. Chalis now helps other people start their own scholarship funds, and is beginning to do this work full time. Her company Philanthropy LLC is changing lives every day. Not only has a *life-giving* situation helped fulfill her, but along the way it has given positive energy to others (scholarship recipients and their families), as well as to those who have continually committed to the scholarship fund. Chalis' scholarships are now endowed, by this I mean they will generate income on their own and can only go up in value.

Life giving does not just apply to work. Work is the most discussed topic because our jobs take up so much of our time. I have seen hobbies and external commitments that were intended to be fun and act as a positive outlet go on to drain life. For example, I am a member of Toastmasters. Toastmasters is an international organization dedicated to improving people's public speaking skills. It has always been *life giving* to me as it allowed me to try out speaking material, and, more importantly, get away from my work and academic life. I wanted to have fun with people who are as crazy and kooky as I am. This held true until I decided to assume the presidency of a club. Suddenly, I was inundated with e-mails, district requirements, and became obsessed with meeting our club goals so we could be considered a top tier club. My fun hobby soon turned into a draining, unpaid job. I decided to step away from the presidency, and focus on my family and activities I enjoyed. As an aside, I made sure there was adequate transition time from me to the next president, and the club was in excellent shape when I left. I have some sense of responsibility. In the years since, I have found ways to give back to Toastmasters, however not as an officer. That has also proved to be life giving for me.

How do we determine what is *life giving?* If you aren't sure, it often helps to start with what we know *isn't*. In the activities section of this book, I have provided several different exercises to help you understand this concept a little deeper, and identify life-giving endeavors on both a professional and personal level.

Resilience.

No endeavor in life is without its challenges. Even the most life giving and satisfying of jobs will have difficult times. It's part of the process; it's part of the fun. This third element in the 'so-happy' formula is *resilience. Resilience* deals with the ability to keep progressing towards a goal no matter how tough the circumstances. As Sylvester Stallone's character, Rocky Balboa, says in the film *Rocky Balboa*:

"Life is about how hard you can get hit and keep moving forward. How much you can take and keep moving forward. That's how winning is done."

To utilize another boxing quote, Mike Tyson once said, *"Everybody has a plan until they get punched in the mouth."*

Both quotes ring true. In the early stages of making our dreams happen, we are excited and enthusiastic. Conquering the world is within our grasp until that first setback happens. At that point we have to reach deep down and find the fortitude to keep going. Many of us don't do that, however. We come across a setback or obstacle, and we either quit or slow down our progress. As we slow our progress and effort, we see the goal slip away. This causes us to slow even more until eventually we have abandoned our efforts. If this happens too often in our life, we learn to have no coping mechanism for adversity and we end up with low *resilience*.

How do we build *resilience*? I have four simple concepts I use to build *resilience*. For me, having a physical challenge and playing college football was the ultimate gut check for me. It was the equivalent of getting my PhD in *resilience.* I relied on these four concepts to get me through it and integrate them into my daily life: hall of fame, celebrate small wins, join the Jedi, and embrace the process.

Hall of Fame.

We've all been successful at several things in our life. We are far more expert than we give ourselves credit for. As a defensive coordinator, I remember being upset after my team's first shutout victory because there were some fundamental errors I saw in the game. Even though we had won 35-0, I focused on missed tackles and a few big plays my defense let up instead of the fact that our opponent had not scored on us. I was focusing on the negative. It took me a long time to break that mindset, and the easiest thing for me to do was to start cataloguing my accomplishments. Thus, when times were tough, I had a quick way to remind myself that I had overcome challenges in the past, and that I possessed the skill to be successful. Create your own *Hall of Fame*. What goes into it?

- Major awards, promotions, accolades, degrees etc.
- Testimonials and e-mails from clients, friends, coworkers etc. that speak to your ability
- Examples of times you overcame a challenge
- Photos and quotes representing your successes

Like any reputable body, induct new moments and members into your *Hall of Fame* on a regular basis. As new successes come up, add them to the Hall. A celebration ceremony is optional and highly encouraged.

Celebrate Small Victories.

We are in a "dream big/think big" culture and for the most part . . . I love it. Going after the big lofty dreams is what pushes us to be better than we ever imagined. The only drawback to this mentality is that focusing on our major goals causes us to forget the small milestones along the way. One of the key moments for me in my football journey came one week into training camp. After several terrible days of testing and struggling on the field, I considered quitting. Maybe I was out of my league in college football. I decided to tough it out and stay for at least one more practice. It was at that practice that I got two sacks on the quarterback. All of a sudden there was hope . . . a glimmer of light that said I could play at this level. That day, I celebrated that victory, and you had better believe it made my *Hall of Fame* immediately. Whenever I had a bad day at practice, I would recall it. I was far off from fulfilling my dream of playing college football, but that day I celebrated a small win that was essential to making it happen: making plays. There would be other small victories I would acknowledge on the way to fulfilling my dream.

Join the Jedi

Or perhaps you could train to be a Sith Lord. I started this book with "Who's your Yoda?" and in continuing with the Star Wars analogy; we need to recruit not just one Jedi Master, but a whole team of them. Mentoring is a key part in building *resilience* and being *so happy* for two reasons. First, when you have people who can mentor you, then you often will see that challenges and setbacks are not that big of a deal. They are part of the process. I remember the first time I totally bombed on stage. I was terrible. The audience didn't react to anything I did. Nobody laughed at my jokes. My emotional moments fell flat (with several audience members looking at their phones constantly). After the speech people stood up and walked away. No thank you. No moments of inspiration. It was all terrible. I called up a speaking mentor of mine (Hank) who always gave me brutally honest answers. After listening to my story, Hank offered me some very solid and practical advice: "Not every speech is going to be a home run. You're going to stink it up sometimes. It's ok. Learn from it and move on." I immediately put the experience behind me and continued on my speaking journey.

Second, recruiting mentors and learning from them is in itself a *life-giving* process when you surround yourself with people who are committed to assisting you in attaining your dreams and have lessons to teach you. No matter where you are in the process, having mentors to help you along the way will keep you focused. Mentors have been in your situation before and can give you valuable advice on how to deal with it.

Recruiting mentors can seem difficult if you don't have a lot of experience in an area but it is quite simple. Begin by reaching out to people who have been successful in your area, and read about others who have been just as successful. Some mentoring relationships will not be a one to one teacher-to-student relationship. It may be one or two phone conversations, and that's ok. I have found over the years, people are generally helpful and open to giving advice if you aren't asking them for a job or selling them a product or service. Eventually, you will find a few mentors who you can bounce ideas off of or go to for advice on a more consistent basis. In the case of some professions, formal mentoring programs exist. In higher education, there are mentoring programs for aspiring senior officers, members of particular affinity groups, and even for new professionals. Take advantage of these types of programs whether they exist through your employer, your professional association, or even in your community. Remember, the Jedi employed a communal approach to training and so should you.

Embrace the Process.

Quite often we see things in black and white, success and failure. Hitting targets and goals is important, but there is a process to aid you that goes beyond hitting a statistical measure. The process is simple, and it goes like this:

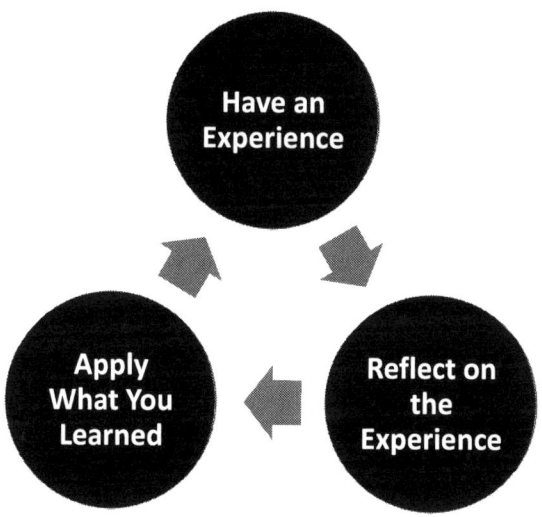

A commitment to this continuous cycle builds *resilience* because it takes away the win/lose binary and puts the emphasis on continuous improvement.

Let's say you have the goal to make an extra $1,500/month as a life coach. That's your goal. You hit the target in month one, but you fail to hit it in your second month. There are a few ways to take on this setback.

1) Decide life coaching is not for you and quit.
2) Decide it was a bad month, and just keep going doing the same thing you were doing.
3) Analyze why you failed to hit your monthly target. Discuss the challenges with a mentor if you can. Apply the lessons learned to the next month and move forward.

The first two options don't allow you to grow and move forward, the third one does. If you chose option two you could be correct that perhaps it was just a "slow" month, but you run the risk of blaming external events versus focusing on what you can control. To be honest, even if you exceeded your monthly target option three is still the best option. For example, let's say your goal is still to make $1,500 as a life coach. You hit your target in the first month, and in month two you make $2,700. Your options are to:

1) Decide life coaching is for you and keep going doing the exact same thing you are doing.
2) Decide life-coaching is for you and keep going doing the exact same thing you are doing and see if there is a pattern.
3) Analyze why you exceeded your monthly target. Discuss this with a mentor if you can. Apply the lessons learned to the next month and move forward.

It could be that you have stumbled on a system that works for you and generates revenue. Great! Fantastic. The question then becomes: how do you know? How will you track this? If business begins to dip how can you assess it? How will you adapt?

Resilience is as much a commitment to this process as having some sort of internal drive to keep going. It's more of a mindset. The key to mindset is continually seeking feedback and learning. When this occurs, then wins and losses aren't as important as improvement. Your happiness increases and after a while challenges stop becoming challenges, and start becoming opportunities for growth.

To build your *resilience* building muscle, the activities section of this book will have exercises ready to help you in this area.

CHAPTER 3: BEAR AND YAK

The cold Michigan air greeted me as I walked through the airport doors. Even though my car was nearby each step was summoning what little energy I had left. I was exhausted from the conference, and even more exhausted by the virus that seemed to be getting worse. I just wanted to go home and sleep in my own bed. It was 11:45 pm and I knew Alessio would not be awake. Still, I planned to sneak a peek in on him if I could.

While my body was tired, my mind was still racing a million miles per minute. The conference had been stimulating and challenging on so many levels. There were aspects of my career that I loved such as analyzing and writing policy, giving advice to groups, and of course the speaking and training. Those things energized me. The question was; did I do enough of those things in my job to sustain me?

My mind kept coming back to the answer *no*. I looked at my career trajectory as a future VP and those things would also disappear; especially the training and speaking. I would probably do more of the policy stuff, but would that make me happy or as Alessio would say, *so happy?*

I arrived at the house, crept up the stairs, and cracked open the door to Alessio's room. I just wanted a glimpse of the little man resting even if it was in the dark. I tried to focus on his bed, but couldn't see much.

Inspired by my love of 1980's Ninja films, I nimbly took a few steps closer to him. I could now see the bright colors of his comforter set . . . but no Alessio.

I took one more elongated step forward before craning my head over his bed. In the middle of the bed lay a large mound comprised of blankets, pillows, and stuffed animals. At the top of the mountain was a very plush and worn out brown teddy bear. I knew somewhere beneath that heaping mountain was Alessio. He had to be there! After all, I could hear him snoring.

Aided by just a smidge of moonlight, my eyes began to adjust to the room. The bear become more pronounced as did the rest of Alessio's entourage: Bunny, Puppy, Ducky, and of course the infamous Monkey whose smirk was always mocking me as if to say, "I get to play with your son more than you ever will."

I couldn't see him but I knew my son was smiling and content. Aside from Sherri (and me on rare occasion) Alessio hung out with those stuffed animals on a daily basis. They were not just his friends, they were his joy. Especially Bear, who was often given a seat at our dinner table and was required to travel with us to all destinations. We had once forgotten Bear at my parent's home in Toronto after a holiday visit. Needless to say Bear was shipped to us via UPS overnight delivery. Bear travels better than I do.

Alessio also had one totally non-plush toy friend who was completely imaginary: Yak. Yak was well . . . a yak and a tiny one at that. Yak fit in the palm of Alessio's hand and was often the cause of spirited conversation. At first the discussions were pleasant, and I would hear my son say things like "Yak funny." So much so that it became common for me to hear things like: "No, Daddy. You no talk to Yak."

At some point however, things started turn. Alessio would scold Yak for doing something wrong and would then teach him the right way to act.

"No Yak! No steal!"

"No Yak! Don't eat my crackers. Time out!"

The lessons didn't seem to stick after a while until one day I realized Yak was gone. I was curious. I asked Alessio where Yak was.

His reply: "Yak go away. He bad."

Alessio didn't seem bothered however because he had Bear and his crew to keep him happy. And that's the thing, he was happy! Bear and Bunny and whomever were the constant source of smiles, hugs, and laughs. They enhanced his life so he kept them around. Yak did not and Alessio kicked him to the proverbial curb.

It was that easy.

*** The Lesson ***

Perhaps Alessio's associations were only with stuffed animals and imaginary friends but the fact that he only associates with things that make him happy needs to be noted. Have you ever notice how children cry, hit (I know it's a no-no), and run away from adults or other kids they don't like? They trust their instincts even if it is at the expense of your Aunt Lorraine who just wants a kiss. There's some basic wisdom in that, especially given the fact that as adults we often subject ourselves to being around others who may not fulfill us, and, in some cases, (often work related) bring us down.

We need to rid ourselves of the Yaks and focus more on the Bears, Bunnies, and Monkeys of the world.

Of course, to say that we should just label people as bear or yak may seem simplistic and sometimes is easier said than done. Remember, Yak presented himself as a friend to Alessio before showing his true dastardly nature. Indeed, there are some negative influences in our lives that are easily identifiable. They are the equivalent of the classic movie villain complete with a trench coat and long moustache to twirl. Although those villains are rare, if they exist in your life then you need to get get rid of them immediately. For other instances, here are some other signs to watch out for that could be potentially bringing you down:

The Over-Persuasive Yak.

You know the type of person who at first you enjoyed talking with, but the more you engage with them the more you realize it's all about what they want. A telltale sign of the over-persuasive Yak is that they will argue, and try to convince you even when you agree with them. These types of relationships can be taxing and unnecessarily combative.

The Selective Hearing Yak.

This Yak appears to be a great friend as well. They aren't usually bad people either, but any time you have a problem . . . they usually aren't listening. You open up your heart, make yourself vulnerable, ask for advice and what you get most of the time is one of two responses: deflection or de-escalation.

Deflection occurs when there is no true response to your issue. You may get a "that's unfortunate" before the subject quickly turns to one of their problems. De-escalation is slightly better because what you have said has been acknowledged, but it is quickly de-escalated so that your "friend" can tell you how much better/or worse they have it. In debt $15,000? Well your friend will tell you they are in debt $20,000. Excited about a new promotion? Well your Yak friend's partner just got a more lucrative promotion. In both cases you are never really validated which means you need to move on.

The Unsatisfied Yak.

This Yak (also referred to the *Naysaying Yak* in some parts of the world) exists only to tell you that your achievements weren't that great, and that you won't be able to get to the next level. When I was pursuing my football dream, I would hear things from a friend like, "You will never survive training camp."

I survived training camp.

"Ok, fine, but you will never make the dress list."

I made the dress list.

"You won't play in a game."

I did . . . and on it went. Whenever I achieved a goal it was minimalized and a new bar was set. There is no pleasing this Yak, and nothing you do will ever get them to admit they were wrong. Move on.

The Dramatic Yak.

This Yak takes on several different forms, but at their core they love to gossip and revel in drama. Sometimes it is real over-the-top, Real Housewives of Yak Vegas, flip over the table and throw the wine in your face type drama. More often the Dramatic Yak tries to pull you in to the day-to-day gossip. This can be quite toxic as you begin to feed off this negative and unproductive energy. Be especially careful of this yak when you and your coworkers are in toxic work situations. What you think is a healthy venting session or a way to cope with turbulence at work can quickly morph into a negative gripe session.

Distancing yourself from this behavior can be difficult because you like these coworkers and you want everyone to be happy. Unfortunately, staying in this mode for too long will only worsen your feelings towards work and keep you in a negative mindset that will cloud positive solutions.

The Jerk Yak.

I cannot think of a better name for this Yak, and the truth is sometimes we just associate with jerks. They're crude, they're not nice, and for whatever reason we don't part ways. We don't even distance ourselves when they insult or belittle us. A colleague once asked me if I would be interested in speaking for his group. I said yes and told him my fee. He replied with "You're not worth that. I'll give you X." He was miraculously surprised when I turned down the speaking engagement and stopped associating with him. By the way, it wasn't about the money, I just didn't like how I was treated.

In contrast to the Yaks, there are all the great Bears that enrich your life. I get excited to talk to the Bears, and talking to them usually brings out countless hours of laughter and buffoonery. Like Alessio's crew, there are many different types of Bears to incorporate into your life. Here are the three I think you need to look out for and keep around.

The Challenging Bear.

Surrounding yourself with good people does not equal being around "yes" people. I put this Bear first because even though my friends are entertaining to be around, they all challenge me to be better when push comes to shove. If I have an idea or a dream, they know how to maintain the line between being supportive and being constructively critical. Ultimately, they reinforce my decision to move forward with my goals. In some cases, they help me see a better path. It's a win-win for me either way.

The Laughing Bear.

If the company you keep can't make you laugh, raise your spirits, and lighten your mood then why keep any company at all? 'Nuff said.

The Listening Bear.

I know this sounds corny, but we need people to listen to us. I mean truly, deeply, authentically listen to us. Good advice is great, but someone who can just sit and listen is essential. We will all need outlets to vent to at some point.

The people we associate with are instrumental to our success. We have all heard the cliché *you are what you eat* and *you are who you hang out with.* I prefer the lesser known cliché of *show me your five best friends, and I will show you who you really are.* Thus, who are you and who are your friends? Ask yourself:

1) Who do I surround myself with?
2) Do I associate with those that make me smile and laugh?
3) Are my relationships positive?

4) Can my friends offer me advice in a way that doesn't belittle me or bring me down (can they be constructive, but not destructive?)
5) If others bring me down do I distance myself from them?
6) Am I bold enough to eliminate them completely?

In relation to question six, if you can't eliminate them (or don't want to) then reframe the question as: If I can't say goodbye, then how do I say hello less often?

For exercises on how to identify the Bears and Yaks in your life go the activities section of this book.

Create-a-Yak

Draw and label your own YAK (or Bear).
Tweet @PaulArtale and #2yearoldsguide to
share it!

CHAPTER 4: NO!

Seeing my son asleep was better than not seeing him at all. I didn't stay in the room long, but took pleasure in the fact that we would play in the morning. Mornings were usually fun and Alessio was at his most entertaining right after he woke up.

I collapsed into bed trying carefully not to wake Sherri. I let out a deep sigh, and didn't have much trouble falling asleep. I was dead to the world. I woke up to sunlight seeping through my bedroom window, the smell of pancakes, and an empty house. I had slept through Alessio's morning ritual and antics. Later on, Sherri would tell me he poked at my eye, but I would not move. I had missed him again. To make matters worse my stomach bug had me bedridden. I felt terrible. I was having no luck.

I decided to take a sick day to recuperate. I could relax and fill time until my little man came home. The day started rough, but it could still end strong. Besides, a little R&R was good for the work-life balance, right?

In honor of my son, I decided to take an afternoon nap; a nap that was interrupted by my text message alerts. My coworker Gary had messaged me saying there was some trouble brewing with one of the groups (let's call them the Canadian Appreciation Society or CAS) I advised. There is no point in going through the details, but in general I had to uphold a policy (which protected the organization from a lawsuit) and in doing so CAS had to reverse a decision they had made. That made CAS very angry. My relaxation slowly began replacing itself with anxiety and anger. Within minutes my boss had told me to come back to campus by four p.m. as CAS was having a dinner with some high-level administrators in attendance.

Being the dutiful soldier I was, I agreed. I caught a catnap, downed every pill and supplement I thought could help, and drove in to work. The event itself was extremely bland. Students came, they ate, they conversed with the high-level administrators, and they left.

The high-level administrators ignored my existence and CAS said they were glad to see me. An hour after the dinner, those same members of CAS stormed into my office and complained about my decisions, and vowed to voice these complaints to the highest level of administration possible.

The stress and anxiety came back, five times worse than before. I closed my office door, and called my boss Shelly. I began to work on drumming up documentation to prove their reasoning was flat out incorrect, and how I was protecting the university. I was so worried about my reputation that I went into protection mode. I became over-fixated on the situation. Nothing else mattered.

It didn't matter that the reasons they wanted to remove me were fickle.

It didn't matter that most of the campus could care less.

It didn't matter that I would waste so much time preparing to defend my name that my son was asleep yet again by the time I got home.

That's when the switch went on.   That's when I
started to see the error of my logic. That's when I came to
terms with the fact that I wasn't as big and tough as I thought.

One of the keys to negotiating is to not flinch,
generally reject the first offer, and above all else draw a line
in the sand that will allow you to say 'no' without remorse,
and walk away if your minimum terms are not met.

Alessio does this all the time.

"Alessio, want to go to your room and clean up?"

"No!"

"Alessio, do you want to give Nana Gladice a kiss?"

"No!"

"ALESSIO DON'T JUMP ON THE KITCHEN
TABLE!"

"No yell at me, Daddy."

"(whispering) Alessio, don't jump on the kitchen
table."

"No!"

Even though the scenarios are goofy, one thing that
is hard to deny is that children say *no* to anything that they
don't like or are not comfortable with. That's why they

won't eat the broccoli or give Nana Gladice a kiss. Why is saying no so hard for us as adults?

More importantly, why was it so hard for me?

For inspiration, I didn't just think of my son's stubborn nature, but I remembered Sherri's as well. Years ago, Sherri was offered the opportunity to become a department head. They gave her an interim position to start, with the option to make it full time soon after. Within a few days, Sherri could tell the position was not a good fit for her. The situation with her new supervisor was not optimal, the job demands were too stressful. In addition, the deliverables she was being tasked with were borderline unrealistic, and required her to cross some of her own ethical boundaries. When the time came to accept running the department on a permanent basis, Sherri calmly told the company "No."

They were shocked (and very angry). I will be honest, and say even I was disappointed at first. She was letting an excellent opportunity pass her by, not to mention a great pay raise.

In saying *no*, she took some of her control back. She had power in that moment that nobody could take from her. She made the best decision for both Sherri the person and Sherri the professional. I realized then that I always put the needs of the professional me ahead of the personal me. I never say *no* when it comes to work, and although I generally love my life, I know that it came at the expense of relationships and experiences that I couldn't get back. In that moment, it came at the expense of not seeing my son for another twenty-four hours. Something had to change. I needed to say *no* . . . but to what?

There is an inherent power in saying *no*. Saying *no* to things takes back some of the control in our lives or at the very least sets our boundaries. To be clear, the *power of no* should not be confused with being stubborn, not doing your job, or causing trouble just for the heck of it.

The *no* card comes out only when you fully understand your boundaries, your limits, the elements you are no longer willing to accept. *No* is also not just a work principle. Sometimes you need to say *no* to the things in your personal life in order to improve your situation. Years ago, I was heavily involved in several community organizations. I loved the work, but it began to take time away from my family, and started to feel more and more like a job. I slowly decreased my involvement in order to bring balance back to my life.

No matter what realm your *no* occurs in (and it will occur in all of them at some point if you are doing it right), you must think long and hard about what your limits are. Once you define your limits you will quickly see what areas you need to say *no* to.

Now I will acknowledge that life is not always as simple as saying *no*, and a supervisor replying with "Ok! Sorry to bother you."

With that being said, there are levels of control we have in most situations. Even if we can't cut out a habit or stressor completely, we can often manipulate it, and chip away at its harshness. Even these small changes can bring you relief.

Finally, sometimes saying *no* doesn't actually involve saying *no* . . . physically. Sometimes it is just a conscious choice that we are not going to participate in certain behaviors or make a decision to stop doing something. It can be deciding not to move forward with a new job or initiative because we are tuned into what our needs and boundaries are.

During a conversation with my friend Gary, he revealed to me that he once just stopped going to a certain committee meeting because it did not deal with his work directly and it was a drain on his time. Eventually, he formally withdrew. But it began with Gary making a decision to not fill his time with useless and non-mandatory meetings. He was happier and funny enough that the administration didn't even notice. He did eventually talk to his supervisor about why he stopped attending the meetings, and was able to get formally dismissed from the committee.

Before moving on, I want to note that I am writing about the events that occurred with CAS because it is part of my story. I am not trying to discredit the organization or rehash what was a bitter battle at the time. It was a small occurrence in the overall scheme of my professional career as a college administrator, but a major occurrence in how I envisioned the rest of my life. I recognize that *no* as I write this book. When the incident was occurring, it definitely had an enormous and stressful impact on my life. As those events unfolded, I began to observe how people reacted to me, the situation, and the work environment in general.

I can remember calling up my mentors, and explaining the situation to them. I was so angry at the time. My mentor, Chuck, was a partner in major accounting company, and was always my go-to when I wanted a viewpoint from someone not working in education. Chuck was a mover and climber; he was one of the youngest partners in the history of the firm. I decided to tell him the saga. I was expecting to receive some great strategic advice or a fresh new perspective. Instead, what I received was one powerfully blunt statement:

"Paul, why are you wasting your talent with this petty shit?"

I did not have a good answer for him. Chuck knew my passions and desires. He saw my talents. I had told him my dreams, but in that moment his patience was gone. He was demanding that I finally say *no* and walk my talk.

The problem was that when it came to my working life, I was usually afraid to say *no*. My boss would ask if I was able to work on the weekend at the last minute . . . and I would say "Sure! No problem." Extra duties without extra compensation? I couldn't say *no* to that, either. It would be great for the resume, right? The sad part was that I knew what I really wanted all along. I had a firm grasp on the solution to my problem, but I was stuck in the vicious cycle of saying yes to life interruptions and *no* to the life-giving opportunities that constantly presented themselves.

We make that trade off all the time, and repeatedly. Why do we continually do such a thing? There are three central reasons for this. The easiest reason to identify is fear. We're afraid to say *no* to our boss because well . . . the boss signs the check, and we need that money to pay the bills. Sometimes there is a social/societal element. We can't say *no* because our workplace/professional culture would frown upon it if we did. As someone who works in university student affairs, there is an underlying culture that says we are to celebrate 'other duties as assigned.' There are those who wear 'overworked and underpaid' as a badge of honor. If you're working in an environment like that, saying *no* is the last phrase you want to utter . . . at least publicly.

A third reason is we that have a notion that these interruptions are what we want or part of process that will lead to success. *I am an assistant Director . . . this is part of the job and this is what I need to do to move up.* These three reasons hold us back, and can keep us in a state of fear versus a state of passionate enthusiasm. Yet, if we learn to say *no* we quickly discover the power it has.

Before I go further, I want to clarify that I am not advocating for saying *no* to everything or that by saying *no* I want you to do no work. That's not it at all. What I am saying is that, at some point, you need to learn to define and draw your boundaries. Once you have done that, you need to do what you can to protect those boundaries. So let's talk about boundaries. What are they? How do they apply to us? How can we protect them?

What are Boundaries?

For sports lovers, boundaries in an athletics context refer to the lines that mark the official playing field/surface. If a player or ball crosses those lines they are 'out of bounds', and usually there is some sort of penalty or stoppage of play. As children, we are taught about personal boundaries from a physical level. This is the reason many of us in American culture are uncomfortable if someone stands too close to us while talking. We often step back. Why? There has been an encroachment of our boundaries. Our personal space has been violated, and we try to correct it as quickly as we can.

Just like sports and personal space, work-life has boundaries too. These boundaries are internal, but they are crucial to our happiness. Having them, however, is not enough. In addition to understanding our own boundaries, we need to also defend those boundaries, and put ourselves in situations that don't violate our preferences as often as possible. When it comes to boundary management, we have to come to understand two terms: *flexibility* and *permeability.*

Boundary Flexibility refers to our ability to shift our work from one time period to another. In other words, it means going beyond a traditional 9-to-5 arrangement and conducting work (and personal business) at times that allow us to get work done *and* tend to our personal needs. This is where alternative work arrangements such as telecommuting, compressing workweeks etc. come into play. Flexible work environments allow this. My job was not overly flexible, primarily because my workload and work commitments made it difficult to rearrange work locations and measures. It's hard to have a flexible work environment when you have high work demands on your time that includes evenings and weekends.

Role permeability refers to your ability (or inability) to transition from one role to another while present in the same space. It is the ability to deal with personal issues at work and work issues at home. In my situation, my work was permeable as I could deal with personal matters at work (i.e. scheduling a doctor's appointment, following up with a babysitter), but was largely impermeable when it came to dealing with work issues at home. I could handle e-mails from home to an extent, but most of the other issues at work required (whether I thought so or not) that I be physically present to resolve them. It was difficult to shift my work to different times or locations because: 1) certain commitments had inflexible preset times, and 2) because face-to-face resolution was required versus digital meetings or the option of moving a meeting/commitment to a more convenient time. In theory, being at the office allowed some permeability. However, when you are busy with the daily grind of the office, you often lose the ability to switch roles on site.

When it comes to *permeability* and *flexibility,* there is no right or wrong. There is only what works for you. Think of it as spaghetti. You can have your spaghetti raw (bend it just a little and it likely breaks), al dente (firm but cooked enough you can move it), or cooked (so it is highly moveable and shapeable.) For me, I want the pasta fully cooked because I love highly *flexible* and *permeable* job situations. It enables me to perform optimally. Other people want more defined roles and defined times. That's ok too. The problem comes when you want cooked pasta, and all you can get is raw noodles or vice versa. When this happens, we begin to experience frustration, dissatisfaction, and anger. The harmony between our personal and professional worlds begins to crumble.

Ultimately, you have to ask yourself this question: do I want my work and life to be integrated, separated, or do I want it to volley back and forth? Ellen Kossek and Brenda Lautsch's book *CEO OF ME* has a great work-life boundary flex-style assessment in it. The book itself offers a reads the ability to understand how they prefer work and personal life to interact. This understanding begins with a simple initial assessment that is fifteen questions long. Your score on it will tell you if you are an integrator, volleyer or separator.

What do these flex-style types mean?

In short:

Integrators like highly permeable and highly flexible work environments. They thrive on being able to shift from one role to another. Take a work call at home or on vacation? Not a problem. Can I leave work for a few minutes to take care of a house need? Sure thing. Don't give integrators strict boundaries or rules revolving around work commitments. For them, it's all about switching things up on an as needed basis.

Separators are the complete opposite of integrators. There is the work world, the personal world, and the two should never really cross over. Cross over will typically anger a separator as they feel it is an encroachment of their time. Separators also look for a more balance approach (although not exclusively) so that an adequate amount of time is devoted to the personal and professional domains.

Volleyers are a hybrid of the *separators* and *integrators*. They recognize that there are certain times of year, projects etc. that require more of their time. They are committed to long hours and will sacrifice time with family during peak periods. The volleyer commitment is based on the notion that eventually things will settle down/even out, and that at some point more substantial time with family over work will occur. When I used to manage university owned apartments (residence halls), I knew that the one-month period revolving around move-in day (the two weeks prior and the two weeks after) would consume a great deal of my time. Family would not be as prominent, but I knew that two weeks after move-in, I could work a more stable work schedule. I also knew that I would reclaim any of my work hours from the move-in at the holiday break in December because residents were gone for several weeks. Although difficult at times, it was a system that worked very well for me.

You could take the test to determine your flex-style, but I bet just by looking at these descriptions, I am sure one of those three types resonates with you. So ask yourself this series of questions:

1)   Which flex-style do I prefer?

2)   Am I currently in a job/life situation that allows that to happen? If you answer 'yes', then great! If you said 'no', then ask yourself:

3)   How do I get from a job/situation that's imposing an incompatible flex-style on me towards being in a job/situation that aligns with my flex-style preference?

One of the most important techniques (other than finding a new job or situation) when it comes to managing your boundary and flex-style preferences is to consistently practice boundary management techniques. Listed below are five techniques that will assist you in setting up boundaries between yourself, your employer, your friends, and family.

Boundary Management techniques:

1)   *Align your style and your career.* This technique has to come first. Once you know what your flex-style is, you have to think about how your preferences fit with either your current job or the job you want. You have to really reflect and analyze it. It is the crucial first step. Once you have a firm understanding of who you are and what you want, you can move on to the next technique.

2)   *Communicate up front.* This works best from day one, but if you haven't had a talk with your manager about your work-life situation then you need to do so ASAP. This goes deeper than boundary and flex-style (although it is closely

related) and speaks to what you want out of your-work life situation. Please note that the intent of the communication is not to make a list of demands on your supervisor. The objective is to bring clarity and understanding. Even in a job that fits well with your work-life needs, it is still advantageous to have the conversation to let your managers know where you stand. Communication up front is also important because it will allow you to understand where your manager and organization stands. For example, a simple talk on expectations over e-mail or a written agreement on how you intend to work from home one day per week can decrease work-life conflict.

3) Flag the fouls. No matter how great an understanding you may (or may not have) with your work environment, it is important to address situations that violate your work-life and flex-style preferences. Just like a referee in a football game throws the flag when s/he sees a penalty, you need to do the same at work. This is much easier if you have mastered techniques one and two. These flags don't need to be confrontational. A flag shouldn't lead to a fight. I once had a boss who called me on the weekend to ask a few quick work questions. I answered them even though I was a little annoyed. On Monday, I decided to address the issue. I remember opening with "Hey, can we talk about your call yesterday" and before I could get another word out my mouth my boss said, "I am sorry for calling you last night. I totally wasn't thinking. I know you value time with your family on weekends." That was it. We were cool.

4) Define your relationship with your cell phone. I probably waited a good five years before I bought a smartphone. Before that, I had a little Nokia that could only send and receive text messages. I had the phone because I honestly don't call people much. After five years, the Nokia died, and I decided to get a Samsung Galaxy phone. Now with a smart phone, I had to make decisions about how I wanted it to interact with my work-life. Was it going to integrate or separate or volley those worlds for me? I decided to volley it, which means that e-mail notifications from work are not sent to my phone's e-mail folder. When I choose to work via e-mail, I must use the web browser version. This is labor intensive, as I have a seventeen digit password. I only check e-mail when I absolutely need to. Likewise, I declined to have the university subsidize my phone bill, as accepting funds for a work phone means I would be beholden to it to some extent. I did not want that, either. I can switch into the work mode if and only if I want to. Otherwise, my phone serves as a means of entertainment and basic communication. I also make it known that unless it is an emergency, do not contact me for work related reasons. That's me. Those are my boundaries. You have to figure out what you want the role of the smartphone to be in your work-life. Integrating is fine, but it can also overwhelm people and create too much tension for some. There's a reason countries like France and Brazil have passed laws restricting and regulating companies contacting employees after hours using smartphones and other means of digital communication. You may not agree with the approach, but the premise is clear enough: digital communications have the opportunity to negatively impact people. Thus, it is crucial for you to understand how you and technology will mesh.

You also need to understand how technology and your job interface with each other. You won't be able to set the boundaries in all situations. Job expectations can force integration in many cases. For example, you want to become a real estate agent because the thought of creating your own schedule appeals to you. As an agent, you *can* have some great flexibility, but it is not guaranteed and can be difficult to systematize. Serving your clients may require taking calls, texts, and e-mails at odd hours. You may have demanding clients who will push your boundaries, and you will have to choose between delivering fantastic customer service and protecting your personal space. It's not easy and the case of so many solopreneurs (aka those who are a one-person business) technological communication is the gateway to this.

Saying *no* and setting boundaries are two powerful weapons you need in your work-life arsenal. Much like a Jedi lightsaber, these weapons are simple. Yet, they are only effective after a great deal of training and mastery

Want to work at mastering your boundary setting skills? Make sure to visit the activities section at the end of this book.

A Pair of 2-Year-Old's Tips:

1) Consider buying a penalty flag and throwing it any time someone in your life violates your work-life boundaries. People will likely think you're odd but you'll have so much fun doing it!

2) Take your cell phone out to dinner and a movie. Have a heart-to-heart, define your relationship, and try the veal.

CHAPTER 5: DO THE VOICE!

I was up early for work the next day. At that point, the stomach virus was secondary to the anxiety and stress I felt. I wanted to take another day off, but I had a "crisis" to manage and a bunch of other work to do. The house was silent as I left for work that day. I watched my family at rest and for a moment I found peace. Tonight was not slated to be a late night. I might actually get to interact with my son while he was awake. At this point I realized that I had more interaction with my family while I was away in Nashville than I did since being back home.

Messed up, right?

The workday went longer than expected, but I managed to get home before bedtime. I sat in the driveway watching the garage door slowly open. In my mind, it was taking forever. I expected Alessio to meet me at the door with hugs, kisses, laughs. Instead, all I could see when I entered the house was the cat sniffing some scattered Cheerios on our dark brown hardwood floor. I could hear commotion upstairs so that is where I headed. I started to ascend when at the top of the stairs, dressed in nothing but a diaper and a blue terry cloth bathrobe that hung open was Alessio.

There was no shouting of "DADDY!" and there was no running towards me. He stood there like a statue and stared through me.

"Alessio!" I greeted him loudly.

Silence. He focused his eyes on me until finally he smiled. I climbed the stairs two at a time and scooped him up into my arms. If there was ever a moment where I turned into an overbearing/over loving parent this was it. I squeezed him to the point where both Alessio and Sherri told me to put him down and let him go. My son grabbed me by the hand and led me to his room to play with his toys. I grabbed a plush Spiderman and started on an adventure.

The adventure, however, was short lived and stopped the minute my phone vibrated with an alert. It was work. I don't remember what it was about, but I do remember that it wasn't urgent and that I paused my time with my son to deal with it. We were in the same room physically, but mentally I was back on campus. Alessio was getting annoyed with me. He put Bear into my hand.

"Daddy play."

My eyes remained locked on the screen of my phone. I held Bear in one hand and texted with the other.

"DADDY PLAY!"

That was enough for me to at least acknowledge him again. I bounced Bear around.

"Hello, my name is Bear. Let's go on an adventure." I said in a pretty unenthusiastic way.

"DO THE VOICE!"

At that point I stopped what I was doing. I put the phone in my pocket and took a deep breath.

"Hey there Alessio, baby, let's go on a hunka hunka burning adventure." I said in my best Elvis Presley impersonation. That's right, in our world Bear speaks like Elvis. All the animals have distinct voices that I use when we play, and they are all based on terrible celebrity impersonations. Bunny is Hulk Hogan, Puppy is a very terrible Sylvester Stallone, Ducky is Barry White, and Monkey . . . well Monkey doesn't get a voice. He creeps me out. Screw him.

Within seconds I became immersed in our little game. Alessio would give me scenarios and I would act them out. Usually the story involved the characters going to a store or sporting event, and ending the day with milk and cookies at Bear's house. The crazy stuff happened in between. At that moment I became totally present with my son, and before I knew it an hour had passed and it was way past both our bedtimes.

** *The Lesson* **

As I lay in bed later that night, I realized my son had revealed yet another pearl of wisdom. *Doing the voice* flipped a switch in me that allowed me to forget about work and have fun. I rediscovered the power of play. Quite often we are told to take up hobbies that relieve stress. The problem I see is that many treat relieving/reducing stress as if it is a medical condition that won't go away, but can be managed. We are not encouraged to play. I will admit I was the kid who played with his action figures until he was twelve years old. It was fun! It still is. I still own those figures!

Playing is the ultimate tool in getting us to switch our minds from work to fun. Alessio asking me to *do the voice* was his way of calling me out. He wanted me to fully engage in play and not just go through the motions. Ever since that day, I have made it a point to incorporate play into both my work and personal life.

If you get a chance, please Google 'The Fish Philosophy'. Fish Philosophy centers around the crew at Seattle's Pike Place Market, and how they play and have fun at work. At the heart of it is a culture that is light, friendly, and incorporates the customers. Whether it is tossing fish around or putting on small skits with them, the folks at Pike's

Place Market have mastered having fun at work. On a personal level, I make frequent trips to toy departments. Sure it is under the guise of looking for stuff for my kids, but I am really there for myself (most of the time). Whether it's toys, video games, going to the park, playing is central to my life right now – thanks to my son.

The problem I see is that we in society are often made to believe play is something that we should not do as adults. It's not as accepted. Some instances where it is accepted is either in a competitive context or as a hobby. Rarely is play for the sake of play actively encouraged. For adults play is also seen as something you do to unwind on your free time – if you have free time. Dr. Stuart Brown is the National Institute for Play. I became aware of Dr. Brown when watching his TED talk. One line in particular grabbed my attention:

"Play has a biological place like sleep and dream."

In other words, play is part of who we are and is essential to our health. Add playtime to the cliché that an apple a day keeps the doctor away (or in my Italian family, a glass of wine a day keeps the doctor away . . . and cures most illnesses). Play is not something we do *if* we have the time, it is something we should do because we *create* the time. Think of how packed our daily lives are. Meeting after meeting, rushing to get from point A to point B, you get home, and you might do something fun that hopefully is not interrupted by work via text, e-mail or call. We have to stop thinking that play is an add-on.

Hobbies and interests are very important, but they can also take us away from a playful mindset if a) you are not careful and b) you mx your hobby with business/competition. Let me give you an example. Earlier I mentioned that I competed in the World Championships of Public Speaking (and in 2018 placed in the top 30 out of over

32,000 contestants. Go me!). I entered the speech contest because I wanted to be a better speaker and because I have fun doing it. Speaking brings out my playful side and competing often enhances it…to a point.

In both 2013 and 2018 (the two years I competed), the fun of competition began to tarnish as I my obsession with winning took over. I would visit several venues per week to practice my speech. I would analyze film of me speaking religiously and I would fixate over changing a single work or sentence for days on end. As the process deepened the competition felt more like a job than play. Noticing this, I made my last two weeks before the competition as fun as possible by trying new jokes, engaging in conversation with my audiences, and actually taking time to enjoy all the cool places I was travelling to practice.

What's my point? Hobbies can often be the only form of play we get as adults and that's ok as long as the hobby doesn't morph into something that stresses us out or turns into another duty. Keep the fun….fun!

I contrast that with playing with Alessio (kids really are the best way to access this part of us) or the times when my creative dramatic side emerges and I begin to improvise jokes and situations around friends. As a kid, I would pretend to be Hulk Hogan or He-Man, in those improvised moments I turned into a character and energetically react to the surroundings. The cool thing is that my friends (because they are whacky like me) joined in, and suddenly there is this incredibly fun and playful energy around us. It's spontaneous and several shades of awesome . . . and yet I struggle to bring that joy into my daily life.

It takes a two-year-old to remind me of it, and he does so with me resisting the whole time.

The reminder to play is crucial in preventing us from engaging in self-destructive behaviors when our daily grind stresses us out. When we are caught up in the daily grind, we are looking for ways to medicate our stress versus treat and eliminate it. That's why we often turn to self-sabotaging behaviors when we are stressed. Bad day at work? Have some ice cream. Fight with your partner? Grab an adult beverage . . . or in some cases go on Tinder (not that I endorse this). Stress and dissatisfaction tends to pull us down into dark and unpleasant places.

We need constant reminders to play because our jobs give us consistent messages to do the opposite. Work environments can often stifle fun as we are under demands to produce and perform. The good news is more companies (including large established companies) are trying to incorporate fun into their culture. At Mastercard's New York office, employees will travel from one meeting to another using a scooter while other areas in the building have pop-a-shot machines or foosball tables.

I enjoy CLIF bars (this is not a paid advertisement) and will enjoy them even more so now that they have a Come Out to Play Campaign that encourages kids, and parents, to go outside and have fun in its many forms. Ice cream giant Ben & Jerry's creates a dog friendly work environment for their employees. Many other companies try to create this culture by having excursions, themed days, contests, and the option to participate in fun events like bowling tournaments or salsa (dancing and food) competitions.

Although working for an employer that believes in fun is definitely something to look for when searching for a job, the responsibility for increasing the play factor in your life starts and ends with you. If you are having trouble recalling what play looks like, remember there are six types of play I want to highlight.

Six Types of Play (in no particular order)

Active play involves movement and physical activity. Examples include tag, laser tag, and chasing your half-naked two-year-old son down the street (or so I have heard).

Cooperative play occurs between yourself and a group of friends. Remember to play nice.

Creative play is play that fires up your imagination and makes you create something out of nothing. This is particularly true when we play with toys, draw, etc.

Dramatic play is about pretend and make-believe. As kids, we did this all the time. As grown-ups, we tend to not see this unless we are involved in the theatre, cosplay, and other adult endeavors. Improv classes are pretty popular these days. You can always try those.

Manipulative play engages your hand-eye coordination and motor skills. Think LEGOs, video games, and building with tools here.

Quiet play is pretty much what it sounds like: play that encourages us to be reflective and focused. Parents love it when their kids engage in quiet play activities such as reading so that we can engage in quiet play such as sleeping . . . I mean, reflective meditation.

I should note that research typographies involving play center around children. This doesn't matter, however, as they are still applicable to adults. The types of play listed above can be useful when we are having difficulty reconnecting with our playful selves. The list can serve both as a reminder of what your options are as well as inspire you to try an activity that you may have not done in a long time or ever. Engaging with my children allows me to participate in dramatic play, something that the former high school theatre nerd in me loves. I am not a very tactile guy, but playing with LEGOS is a lot fun and gets my creative synapsis firing. For those that may think adults playing like children is lame, then think of other activities that are pure enjoyment for you and use that as your play activity. Video games, attending a convention, crafts, taking an enrichment class, whatever it is, the lesson is: engage!

To participate more with this concept please visit the activities section of this book. Doing the voice is optional . . . sort of.

Play with Legos!

So if you play with LEGOS (or any off-brand block interlocking system) and create something cool, make sure to tweet me @PaulArtale and #2yearoldsguide

CHAPTER 6: WHAT HAPPENED?

I was in the middle of an intense story. Bear and Spiderman were arguing over whether to have cookies or pizza during the sleepover at Panda's house. Bear was pro-cookie while Spiderman was all about the pizza. The debate was ping ponging back and forth and tempers flared. At the request of my son, the issue should be settled in the most logical way: football. I scooped up the menagerie of stuffed animals and sorted them into teams. Bear's team consisted of Panda, Yogi Bear, and Monkey. Team Spiderman featured the talents of Papa Smurf, a stuffed giraffe, and a Care Bear (it was Birthday Bear for those who must know). I lined the toys up on Alessio's green play-carpet and the game began.

As a former football coach I actually had the two teams in formation. Bear's Team was more of a run heavy offense while Spiderman loved to throw the football. The two sides battled for hours (it was probably like 10 minutes) until it finally came down to the final play of the game. Team Spiderman needed to score to win. Alessio sat in the middle watching intensely as Birthday Bear sprinted from left to right and back again. Spiderman hiked the ball and Bear came right after him. Papa Smurf tried to block, but Bear grabbed him by his beard and threw him to the fifth row of the bleachers. Spiderman scrambled to his right, and saw Giraffe wide open in the end zone. Yogi and Panda were trying to defend, but Giraffe was just too tall for them. Spiderman planted his back foot and got ready to throw at the exact moment Bear crushed him from behind.

FUMBLE!

Monkey recovered the loose ball and Bear's team had secured the victory! The crowd went bananas (pun fully intended). Alessio looked at me with a puzzled expression on his face. A rare moment of silence ensued until finally, with his had cocked slightly to his left and his little eyebrows furrowed, he asked:

"Daddy?! What happened?"

I took the next few minutes explaining to him the concept of a well-timed blitz and the finer points of fumble recovery. Teaching the intricacies of football truly is a sacred moment in our father-son relationship. Alessio's response was:

"What?"

I explained it again. This time I added a piece about blocking for the quarterback and proper tackling form (which I demonstrated using the toys). Once again he bellowed:

"What?!"

I decided to go with a simple explanation. "Spiderman fell down." He accepted that.

It was at that moment of triumph that Sherri walked in and told us it was time for bed. Having finally explained the outcome of the game to my son, I decided to quit while I was ahead.

Sherri began the evening routine with Alessio while I went downstairs to work on some meaningless proposal for work.

My house backs onto a cute little pond. My evening ritual most nights is to watch/listen to the water while I write. It's something I absolutely love about this house. Sherri adored it because of our large walk-in closets. I loved it because of the pond and all the other soothing aspects of it: rippling water, a beautiful fountain, cool birds (we have a crane that visits frequently and swans on occasion), and even fish. When I first moved here, my evening ritual consisted of writing articles and dissertation notes by the water. The last year however, found me working on e-mails and reports for work. Half the time I wasn't even paying attention to the pond. I asked myself:

"What happened?"

Just two years before that moment I had a plan and I had momentum. My speaking business was picking up, my day job was an extension of my speaking and training skillset. Thus, I had time to spend with my family, friends, and passion projects. Every day was different and that excited me. Now, that was no longer my reality. It's not as though I woke up one morning and my perspective was different. The shift from enjoying life to feeling stuck and miserable occurred one inch at a time. It crept up gradually. Hundreds of tiny moments that I allowed (by not enforcing my boundaries), tasks and commitments that didn't give me life became those that sapped my motivation and energy. I put off writing blogs to tend to needless e-mail at night, or volunteered for committees that took me away from the goals that should have mattered most. I was not getting up earlier (or staying up later) on some days so I could get more done with my business, and I used work-life as a false justification for it.

Most of all, I convinced myself I wanted to go down a career path that really wasn't the best future for me. It would not bring out the best version of myself. It detracted from my family, my work, and my dreams. Mixed in that was a false justification of believing that having a child was an excuse to just work, collect a check and focus on my day job. I had demoted my dream to the status of occasional hobby, a feeling that made me feel disgusted upon realization.

*** The Lesson ***

Our biggest work-life enemy is not our boss, our job, or some unfortunate circumstance. Our biggest work-life enemy is ourselves. When we stop moving towards the lifestyle we want and start making concessions, we are betraying ourselves. When we convince ourselves that it will be better tomorrow, but we have to sacrifice today, we are buying into a lie that too often has us looking back with regret. Time is the most precious resource we have, and at that moment I finally conceded that I had managed my time terribly. I was letting the circumstances dictate where my time was going versus me looking at my schedule (and commitments), and telling time where to go. I would engage in a time analysis activity (just like the one you did in Activity 5.2) or conduct a job task analysis, and I would see the deficiencies. Sadly, I did not scale back, I did not say *no*, I did not make the changes.

There is one simple activity for this chapter waiting for you in the activities section of this book.

CHAPTER 7: WHAT YOU DOING?

I didn't get much sleep that night. If my brain can be symbolized as a hamster running on a wheel, then my hamster had decided to swallow a jar of caffeine pills, wash it down with a case of energy drink, and decide it was best to sprint on the wheel all night long. My thoughts did not just focus on what had happened in my life, but kept fixating on where I wanted it to go. Life used to be a lot more. My work used to energize me and now . . . nothing. Was I just going through a rough patch? Was I going through a pre mid-life crisis? At least I had fun playing with my son the night before. That made me feel better.

I sometimes set my phone alarm to songs I love, and that morning, Guns N Roses' *Paradise City* blasted through my room. Nineties rock music helps me get pumped in the morning. I took my phone into the bathroom and I decided it was time for a shave. Sherri was grumbling at me, and I assumed she was talking about the music volume. I closed the bathroom door before lathering up my face. Moments later the door creaked open. Alessio appeared. At least I knew what Sherri was grumbling about. I turned the music up.

"What you doin'?" he asked with his head cocked to the side.

I told him I was shaving so that I could have a smooth face for work. I plopped him onto the toilet seat so he could watch. To this day, watching me shave is something Alessio enjoys doing. I sang along to *Paradise City* (and in doing that realized the green grass in the song had nothing to do with lawn care) moving wildly and bopping my head. I also continued to shave while dancing or at least I tried to when a quick and even swipe under my jawline interrupted my head banging moment. There was a quick, sharp pain followed by a small but steady stream of blood. I reached for the tissue paper, applied pressure and tried to act cool in front of my son.

"Daddy, what you doing?"

I turned towards him, pointed at my cut and said "Fixing my ouchy."

Alessio smiled and leaned forward to kiss the aforementioned ouchy (which is our standard protocol in the house) I somehow Jedi-mind tricked him into a hug instead to avoid any mess.

Luckily the rest of my shave went without any cuts, and after having a quick breakfast with Alessio and Sherri, I headed out to work – the toilet paper still glued to my face. The drive to work was only fifteen minutes and I was hoping that my cut would dry and heal before I got into the office. As I pulled into the parking space the little bloody square of paper fell off my face and another metaphor popped into my mind.

When I cut myself shaving, I did not think twice about finding a piece of paper and covering the wound. My instinct was to stop the bleeding and to keep going forward. That very same instinct was not present in my personal life. I had metaphorically cut myself repeatedly (and in some cases, others had cut me), and my reaction was not to stop the bleeding and heal the wound, but rather tolerate the pain and discomfort. Unlike the nicks and scrapes we get shaving, these cuts were deep and painful. Despite this, there was no positive (re)action to the circumstance and as a result my life only got worse.

*** The Lesson ***

We can't always control what happens to us, but we can control how we react. It's true. The problem is, we often spend way too much time focusing on the past or trying to change elements out of our control versus devising an appropriate and positive response.

For example, I live in Michigan. Michigan can get very cold. When winter comes around, and I am cold I don't spend my time trying to control the snowfall or wind-chill because I can't. Instead, I put on a sweater or turn up the heat in my house. It's an automatic reaction to the situation. I may curse at Mother Nature or pray for better weather, but in reality I know that the only sensible thing to do is warm myself with whatever means I have around me. This holds true for many physical needs (warmth, being dry, protection from danger etc.). We want our thought process and reaction to all situations to be that automatic.

Are all situations as simple as fixing a shaving cut or getting warm when it's cold? Clearly the answer is no. Let's look at another situation that's common to us, but can be a lot more complicated: eating at a restaurant.

Anything can happen when you go to a restaurant. You may have a long and uncomfortable wait to get a table, you may receive bad service, there can be mistakes on your order. Sometimes the food may be anything but delicious. Let's look at the first scenario: having to wait to get a table. Have you ever observed other people when you are in this situation? I have and it is both fascinating and highly entertaining.

The maître'd tells the potential customer that it will be a forty-five minute wait to get a table, and that's where the fun starts. Some people get angry, but still want to stay at the restaurant. They choose to wait and complain about the wait the entire time. Another batch of people will walk out the door almost immediately. Some will choose to use the waiting time to continue conversing and enjoying each other's company. Then there are the analyzers. They look at their watch, poll their colleagues for opinions, weigh the alternatives, and finally make a decision.

Depending on the restaurant, sometimes you will be offered a chance to eat immediately if you are ok with eating at (or in) the bar area. People's reaction to this also varies. I found (from my completely unscientifically proven) observations that many people will wait it out as they are committed to the idea of eating at a traditional table. Thus, many of us choose to be miserable or at least uncomfortable when waiting for a table to open at the restaurant. We could just as easily walk out or eat at the bar, and accomplish our goal of eating sooner than later. The next day, we'll complain about how long the wait was in a subconscious attempt to share the misery.

Unless we are wowed by the food and the service afterward (which brings about a 'it was worth the wait' anecdote to others), we essentially tolerate a less than ideal situation. I am a very impatient person, but in a situation where I have to wait, I will use the extra time to converse, walk around the parking lot or area, or read/watch something on my phone. I won't let something like a wait damper my mood, as I choose not to react negatively.

This analogy takes us to our work-lives where the twists, turns, and turmoil of the work environment can test us on just about every level. Likewise, our personal lives can affect our performance at work. No matter the circumstance, we must keep going. Too often we don't. We remain stuck in a cycle where the only reaction we choose is tolerating the present and hope for a better future. That's what I was doing. Tolerating, however, is not a good solution as it leads to either a) the situation getting worse, or b) the situation gets better but it negatively taints you.

Building the resilience to react is rooted in answering six questions: 1) What can't I control? 2) What can I control? 3) What has actually changed? 4) Has there been announcement of change? 5) What's course of action will I take right now? 6) If events aren't too my liking, what is my exit strategy?

Let's take a quick look at each.

Six Questions to Help Build Resilience

1) *What can't I control?* You should recognize that there are factors out of your control. Decisions in organizations are often made several levels above you or are part of a bigger strategy or philosophy. We all need to recognize that what's done is done in that moment. Most of the elements that we cannot control are systemic and involve authority or power we don't own.

2) *What can I control?* The most obvious reply to this question is your reaction. Reaction refers more to one's behavior than it does one's emotion. When you're in a bad situation you have every right to be angry, sad, frustrated, etc. Letting those emotions guide your behavior, however, is what can keep you in a more positive space. It can be tough to keep performing your job at a high level when you are in a tough situation. Yet, it's a choice you can make. You can choose to involve yourself in office gossip

or the pity party, or you can put yourself into more positive situations. You can also look at what elements of your situation you can control. For example: job duties, decision making power, control of schedule, vacation time and so on. Even after a terrible event, we can always find some elements we can control.

3) *What has actually changed?* The decision comes down from above. You get angry. You decide to keep moving forward in your job and stay away from the gossip gallery. There is a cloud of gloom over the office, but ask yourself in that moment: *what has actually changed?* You may not like that Kevin from accounting has been made Vice-President of finance because he is combative and condescending. He assumed control of the division, but if you can extract the emotion from it, you may found that not much (if anything) has changed aside from the personnel. Sometimes we are reacting to our perceptions rather than the reality.

4) *Has there been an announcement of change?* If the answer is 'no' then revisit steps 1 through 3. If the answer is 'yes', then life gets fun and interesting. The first step is to stay calm and think critically. The second step is not to *over*think. If change has been announced, then take yourself through this quick questionnaire as a means of separating emotion:

  a. *Does the announcement impact me directly?*
  [ ] YES [ ] NO
  b. *Does the announcement impact my supervisor directly?* [ ] YES [ ] NO
  c. *Has the announcement given complete information?* [ ] YES [ ] NO

d. Is the change immediate?   [ ] YES [ ] NO
e. I am excited by this change.   [ ] YES [ ] NO
f. Can I live with this change? [ ] YES [ ] NO

g. Does this change impact me negatively?
   [ ] YES [ ] NO
h. Is this change a deal breaker where I will
   look for work elsewhere?   [ ] YES [ ] NO

5) *What is my course of action right now?* By this point, you have as much information as possible in front of you. Your next step, then, is to think of what you will do in the short term. Even if the situation is terrible, and not to your liking, you will likely stay a little while. Few of us can afford to quit on the spot or turn in our resignation within a matter of days. Conversely, you may love these changes, and are eager to implement them sooner than later. Your course of action needs to be strategic and calculated. The course of action you choose *does not* need to be in line with your emotions and feelings. You can hate what's going on and not agree with it, but your action step can be to help implement it. For example, you may disagree with a hiring decision, but fully assist with the onboarding of that new employee.

Some considerations when making your action strategy are:

a. Would it be helpful to gain further
   clarification from someone?
b. Do I need to get ahead of this change and
   reach out to other individuals/departments?
c. Can I get by just doing my job as it was
   before the change?

> d. *Is there information/data I need to gather and have ready for when the change comes?*
>
> e. *Do I require counseling to cope with the change?*
>
> f. *Do I need some extra training that will make me competent or useful during the change?*
>
> g. *Do I need to investigate other career/job options?*

6) *If the change isn't to my liking, what is my exit strategy?* With all this talk of change, we now need to address the topic of leaving. Sometimes the change is not for the best, and you may deem it not worth muddling through. Our natural inclination is to apply to a bunch of new jobs, and get out as soon as possible. We employ an apply first, ask questions later approach. A successful transition, however, involves a more calculated exit strategy. You have to be strategic and intentional so that you are not jumping from one bad situation to the next. Here is a six step exit strategy process to consider. And yes, this chapter is in love with six-steps. I am aware. Moving on....

Six Step Exit Strategy Checklist

Step 1: Are your materials in order? Don't bother applying if you don't have a proper resume and base cover letter. Make sure the information you have on them is relevant to the job for which you are applying. I strongly suggest keeping a curriculum vita of all your accomplishments so that you can transfer relevant experiences and skills to specific jobs. This will make applying to multiple job types easier.

Step 2: Define Your Destiny. Start doing a search of the jobs you want. I call this step 'define your destiny' because this is the time where you can reflect and decide if this is the type of work you want to do. This is the *So Happy* principle coming back in full force. If you had this exact job in a different work place, would you be content? You should strategically decide if the move you want to make will be a step up the career ladder, or will it be more of a lateral move. Does title matter to you or are you looking more at compensation packages? Are you willing to move? You must really take inventory of all these questions so that you can create a laser focus on your job search.

Answer this question:

The job I am looking for is _____ (job title/job type) with a minimum salary of _____. I am willing to relocate (or commute) within _____ miles of where I currently am.

Step 3: Reach out to your network. If it's time to make a change, then you have to let people know. Reach out to colleagues and contacts, and let them know what exactly you are looking for.

Step 4: Build your network. A proper job transition can take months and sometimes our current network won't be able to come through. It is important to build your network up by attending conferences, networking meetings, and via social media (if that's something you know to do well). It never hurts to grow the networking pool. Use this time to conduct informational interviews or get career advice from contacts. People love to give advice and can provide you with some great tips that can help you.

Step 5. Get your finances in order. If you're looking at leaving, then making sure you have finances in order is necessary. This is essential in general, but if the situation at work is shaky or unpalatable then a strong financial plan has to be at the forefront. In some instances, you may lose your job or see a pay decrease because of the change. In other cases, you may come to a point where the work situation is intolerable and you feel the need to resign. You may need extra funds for job search related expenses (travel is the biggest), and depending on the type of job you accept you may need extra funds for moving expenses.

Until you are on stable ground, you may consider a more stringent budget. If you are not in the habit of analyzing your expenses, you may want to start with a three to six month financial analysis. This will help you target areas of budget you can tighten if needed, and give you an accurate view of what your cashflow is.

Step 6. Be Friends with Feedback. You will get interviews. Opportunities will present themselves. Information will cross your plate. Through it all you have to commit to being friends with the feedback because not every interview will go your way, not every opportunity will work out (or be in your best interest), and information is useless if we don't know what to do with it.

If we get into the habit of applying the feedback and data then we can sharpen our skills and be better prepared for situations that emerge. These situations can be anything from interview questions to analyzing a job offer. You can apply the 3-step process from chapter two. Take a look at the graphic once again to refresh your memory.

Let's go through a quick example with this: a job interview question that caught you off guard but feel will be asked again in subsequent job interviews.

- *Have an experience:* You were asked the question.
- *Reflect on it.* What did you think of the question? How did it catch you off guard? What did you like/not like about your answer? If you want, take it a step further and catalogue the question in a document or database.
- *Apply what you learned.* Write down how you will answer it next time. What's the ideal answer if a question like this emerges again. Review this section before your next job interview.

Apply it next time: Leave this space blank until the situation comes up again. When it does, start the process over again.

To put these lessons intro practice turn to the activities section of this book.

CHAPTER 8: WORK APPLE

Cuts aside, I started my workday at 6:45 in the morning that day. CAS had scheduled a breakfast with the chancellor and had ordered tacos as their meal. As usual, it was up to me to ensure students attended this event. The decision to have tacos was that of the club's president who did it because he thought it was funny despite everybody else disagreeing.

In another work situation, I would have probably stepped in and changed the menu. However, that was not the world I was living in. Thus, we had tacos coming, and a low response rate for the event. I assured my boss I'd be in early to try to drum up support.

At 6:45 am I was scouring the halls of our university center randomly asking people if they'd like tacos for breakfast (I probably should have just used the term "free breakfast" but my mind was not in the most creative space at that time) and a chance to meet with the chancellor. Naturally, the few people that were actually there ran from me like a politician running from a journalist. It was a miserable experience that had me constantly asking myself two questions:

1) *What am I doing with my life?*
2) *Why am I doing this to myself?*

The second question in particular kept running through my head. Yes, I wanted to keep my job. Yes, I cared if the event succeeded (despite my turbulence with the club). Yes, as advisor what happened was a reflection on my leadership. It was all true and yet I didn't have to be there early in the morning and by doing so frightening our students. I was trying to change the outcome in a situation that was already predetermined. To be honest, part of my reason for being there rested in the ability for me to say "I did everything I could" if criticism came my or my bosses way about the event attendance. *IF!* I was making myself miserable based on one hypothetical reaction to an unknown outcome. The breakfast went fine, and all the tacos and burritos were eaten. My day went on without any major incident, and I was even able to leave work early to be with the family.

I pulled into the garage and Alessio was there to greet me. He smiled, he waved, and the minute my engine turned off he ran to my door and demanded to sit on my lap so he could play with the steering wheel. I often don't let him in the front of the car, mainly because Alessio has quick hands and takes great joy in stuffing small objects into the CD player. This time, I decided to let him.

He moved the wheel side to side and even sneaked in a blast of my horn. We were having great fun with this when all of a sudden he stopped. Alessio looked down at my cup holder and pointed at the three apples that were crammed into it. They weren't just any apples, however, they were the *work apples.* Work apples were apples that Alessio gave me on an almost daily basis because he took the lesson of "an apple a day keeps the doctor away" to heart. Let this be a lesson to you all: beware of the clichés you teach your children. They can be used against you.

"Work apple!" he exclaimed. "Daddy no eat!"

I became defensive and tried to concoct the perfect alibi. "Daddy was too busy to eat it Alessio. I get very busy at work and daddy forgets to eat the apples."

In that moment I realized that I was not only lying to my son, but I was also lying to myself. Next to the three apples

jammed into my beverage holder were three Big Mac containers. After a long, rough day at work I would sometimes go to McDonalds and grab a burger or two. I just so happened to be going through a Big Mac phase at that time. The image of the burger boxes and the apples virtually side-by-side became the perfect analogy for my life choices. Here I had this delicious, vitamin filled, healthy piece of food that was at my fingertips daily, and yet every time I was tired, stressed, or even hungry for a snack I opted for the sodium filled, high fat, sugary sauce drenched unhealthy option. I didn't make that choice once but just about every time. A question I asked myself earlier in the day now resurfaced with an even more poignant impact:
Why was I doing this to myself?

*** The Lesson ***

What I learned from that encounter in the car was two very simple lessons. Those lessons are:

1) Stop taking the easy path. Especially when the better path is within a fingertips reach. I could also call this lesson *"stop reverting back to old habits."* More often than not, we know what the right thing to do is, but we choose the less optimal option. *Scent of a Woman* is my favorite film of all time. Al Pacino is brilliant in it. At the end of the movie he gives an incredible speech about integrity. I'll quote part of it here:

> *"Now I have come to the crossroads in my life. I always knew what the right path was. Without exception, I knew, but I never took it. You know why? It was too damn hard."*

To drive that point home further, I remember an interview with Muhammad Ali where he stated how much he hated training and the work that went into becoming a legendary fighter. As much as he hated training, Ali repeatedly told himself:

'Don't quit. Suffer now and live the rest of your life as a champion.'

The right choice is usually not the easy choice. Success requires sacrifice and becoming comfortable with the uncomfortable. You cannot grow and develop if you do not grind and dedicate yourself to success. Success starts with you and the ability to create successful habits is usually at your fingertips. There is no growth without pain.

Let's look at the example of going to the gym. You want to get in shape. You step onto a treadmill and glance at the screen. The screen on a treadmill will ask you two questions: what workout program and what intensity do you want? The choice is completely up to you. You also have the power to increase or decrease the difficulty setting at any time. You can also choose to stop when you feel tired.

The challenge with the treadmill (or any workout program) does not come when you are feeling great and motivated. It comes when the times are tough, when you are feeling sore or flat out lazy. Those are the days where you may elect not even to step onto the machine or if you do, to set it at a more comfortable pace. Those are the days when the last thing on your mind is to increase the intensity and difficulty and by doing so, improve yourself.

Let's take a less physical approach to this concept as well: time. Work-life issues are largely time related. Too much time is being asked of us, drained from us, or being spent in a state of discord. We all wish we all had more time in a day. After doing the time analysis activity in chapter two you will have noticed that you have inefficiencies in your time. The question is: will you make the adjustments? Two of my biggest time inefficiencies are social media and Netflix. I love chatting on messenger and I love binge watching Netflix series or documentaries. It's a source of stress relief for me *until* it keeps me from engaging in more productive and healthy habits. I make the choice to message someone or watching two more episodes of *Orange is the New Black.* This is fine if I have nothing of importance happening. Am I functioning in the optimal zone where I am completing tasks and habits that will benefit me in the long term? I liken it to being preventative versus reactive; treating the root cause versus the symptom.

This is why we must look to the second lesson I learned from the work apple incident:

2) Taking care of our well-being is beyond important in this process. Although health and nutrition is not the focus of this book, I would be remiss if I did not take a brief moment to address that diet and exercise are a vital part of the work-life puzzle. A healthy lifestyle gives you more energy, decreases the chance of illness, and strengthens you. A stressful and negative work experience opens us up into giving into self-destructive behaviors. For some, it is drugs or alcohol, others shopping, and, for people like me, its food. A bad day at work is always made better with a juicy, greasy burger . . . for about three minutes, but oh what a great three minutes it is.

The area of diet is a sensitive area for most. We have an almost intimate relationship with food. Food stirs up emotions in us. If you eat something that is tasty you feel joy. If you eat something your parent makes (or something similar to it), you begin to feel nostalgic and connected to the family and past. That's why I can't say no to my mother's lasagna or for that matter *any* lasagna. For me, it brings up memories of big family dinners and special occasions. Sometimes we indulge, and feel naughty and mischievous. Have you ever gone to a function or come home to a meal filled with food you hate? You experience a plethora of emotions ranging from disgust to utter disdain. In addition, sometimes, when we go off track or engage in making poor food choices, we feel shame. That shame makes us want to hide the habits. We don't talk about it and that can take us into a downward spiral. Food is powerful!

Whereas food typically brings up fun and positive emotions for us, exercise and being active are often associated negatively. Some of us hated gym class and sports which automatically puts us at odds with exercise. Most of us have trouble finding the time to squeeze it in or stress makes us think that. All of us can work 15-30 minutes of activity in daily. It's not that hard, especially break it up over the course of a day. YouTube is filled with an endless amount of 5-10 minute workouts. I personally use *HASFIT* which is free and has hundreds of workouts at all levels and time commitments.

The activity and exercise component is important because the research has been clear about how exercise releases endorphins in our body which makes us feel better, sleep better, and increasing overall happiness.

The best thing you can do for yourself is educate, experiment, and evaluate. This isn't about weight loss – it is about instilling positive health behaviors. Therefore, if you're stressed and feel like there is an imbalance in your wellness then implement the three E's below.

Educate: If something feels off, go learn about how to make it right. If you feel you know enough, then I strongly encourage you to relearn it. There is always an aspect that you will find new or be reminded of in a positive light. Reinforcing our knowledge base can have the same impact as learning a new concept for the first time.

Experiment: Put your knowledge into action. The time to act is now. You have to give the change time to work. As an added bonus, implementing a change (for me anyway) can be exciting and create a lot of positive energy.

Evaluate: Unless otherwise stated through the educate phase, I recommend a ninety-day evaluation period. Research shows that if we do something consistently for ninety days, it has a greater chance of becoming a habit. People often quit their diets between the four and eight week mark. Going in with a ninety day mindset will at least give you a target goal. After the ninety-day period ends, evaluate your progress, what worked, what didn't, and set a new ninety-day goal and start the cycle over again.

In the last chapter, we talked about what we can and cannot control, and that we can always control our reactions to circumstances. The focus was largely on organizational and professional reactions to situations. That is why I feel it necessary to quickly discuss how important it is to be aware of how we react to stress, and the impact those reactions have on our inter and intrapersonal choices.

The chart below contains a list of possible behaviors and choices we may make when something bad happens. It can be related to work or it can be a personal issue as well since troubles in the personal domain often spillover into how you operate at work.

Intrapersonal Behaviors (i.e. stuff we do to ourselves)	Interpersonal behaviors (stuff we do to others)
• Eat poorly • Neglect exercise and activity • (Over)use substances • Stop eating • Oversleep • Isolate ourselves	• Become irritable with others • Withdraw ourselves from situations • Associate with those that are negative and toxic • Neglect commitments

Finally, always remember to keep your total well-being in check. Physical and emotional well-being are important, but so is your spiritual, financial, intellectual, environment, and social well-being. They are all interconnected and need to be tended to. Listed below are seven types of wellness you need to consider in your life.

The Seven Types of Wellness

Social Wellness is the ability to interact with people around you. It involves using good communications skills, having meaningful relationships, respecting yourself and others, and creating a support system that includes family members and friends.

Physical Wellness is developed through the combination of beneficial physical activity/exercise and healthy eating habits. Components of physical wellness include building muscular strength and endurance, cardiovascular strength and flexibility.

Financial Wellness goes deeper than one's bank account. Financial wellness refers to an individual's ability to understand their financial situation, how to navigate the financial landscape, and how to develop strategies for both financial stability and growth.

Spiritual Wellness is a personal matter involving values and beliefs that provide a purpose in your life. Individuals may have different views of what spiritualism is, but it is generally considered to be the search for meaning and purpose in human existence, leading one to strive for a state of harmony with oneself and others while working to maintain a well-balanced life.

Emotional Wellness involves more than just handling stress. It also involves being attentive to your thoughts, feelings, and behaviors, whether positive or negative.

Intellectual Wellness engages in creative and stimulating mental activities to expand your knowledge and skills and help discover the potential for sharing your gifts with others.

Environmental Wellness includes trying to live in harmony with the earth by understanding the impact of your interaction with nature and your personal environment, and taking action to protect the world around you. Protecting yourself from environmental hazards and minimizing the negative impact of your behavior on the environment are also central elements.

There are different tasks on how to us the wellness wheel, and folks like me can do half-day workshops on how to maximize the different aspects of the wheel. The simple first step however, is to look at each aspect of the wheel and ask yourself how well you are doing in each of these domains and then to apply the three E's (starting with evaluation).

Whether your wellness is rooted in choosing the work-apple over a burger, becoming more active, or finding the people and resources to lift your spirit, it is essential that you make wellness a priority. We often let elements of wellness slip during hard times which can take us to dark places. Those dark places can make it difficult for us recognize the next lesson my two year old son taught me.

CHAPTER 9: THANK YOU

BEEP! BEEEEEP!

And at that point the fun in the car was about to stop as Alessio kept pushing down on the horn. The noise didn't bother me as much as I had just replaced the horn due to similar antics he committed a month earlier.

"Ok, buddy, it's time to go." I said as I tried to pry his hands from the wheel.

Alessio wouldn't budge.

I tickled him then pulled.

His grip got tighter, and his shriek transformed into a low guttural grunt.

"Alessio, come on. Daddy's hungry."

The tension in his arms disappeared as he once again looked at the cup holders between the seats. He grabbed a work apple and brought it to my mouth. His devilish grin invited me to take a bite.

To be completely honest, I didn't want to eat the apple. Not because I wasn't hungry and not because I would have preferred another Big Mac but because apples . . . really are not my thing. Definitely not on a daily basis. When it comes to fruit, I am more of a berries kind of guy. I tried to convince Alessio to give me work strawberries…but it didn't work.

I couldn't say no.

I took a bite into what was a nasty, teetering on going rotten mushy apple and sold it like I was biting into the greatest brownie known to man.

"MMMMMMMMMMMM. So good, Alessio. Can I have another bite?"

Alessio's little blonde eyebrows came together in an almost scowl.

"Say thank you!"

I burst out laughing. Over the past few days my son had revealed the simplest and most powerful work-life lessons, and I hadn't thanked him. I was grateful. My attitude had shifted for the better. My son had enriched my life in a way I could have never imagined. He was leading me away from a darker path in life, one quirky moment at a time. I knew he didn't understand that, but I did.

"Thank you Alessio. Thank you so much."

*** The Lesson ***

Up until that moment I had always felt that gratitude was a fluffy, soft practice that had no impact. I am not the most emotional of people so the concept of gratitude never really interested me. I remember rolling my eyes when I was a freshman in college, and many of the people on my floor were writing in gratitude journals because Oprah Winfrey had promoted it on her show. I never saw the benefit in cataloging things you were grateful for. You were either grateful or you weren't, and when something big happened, you'd know to be grateful either way.

I was beyond grateful the first time I put on my college football jersey and by doing so fulfilled a lifelong dream. I was grateful when my wife said "I do." I didn't need a journal for all that.

And you know what? I was right. You don't need a journal or reflection to be grateful for those massive moments in life. It's all those other moments in life that you need a journal for.

Why?

For starters practicing gratitude increases your mental strength. Two studies to note on this are a 2006 study in *Behavior Research and Therapy* revealed that Vietnam War veterans who practiced gratitude had power rates of Post-Traumatic Stress Disorder (PTSD).

In 2003 the *Journal of Personality and Social Psychology* found increased levels of resilience for people following the terrorist attacks on September 11. Focusing on what you have, and what you are grateful for having, even in the most frustrating and darkest of times, is what builds resilience and grit.

Take my situation. Was I miserable in my job? Yes. Did I feel like I was in a rut and underappreciated? You'd better believe it. Do I hate the concept of tacos for breakfast now and forever? Without question.

Was there anything I had to be grateful for during the time of that experience?

Yes, there was.

I was grateful for my boss, Shelly, who supported me through the entire ordeal and defended my actions to administration.

I was grateful for the students who came to my office to voice their disagreement.

I was grateful to Ms. Pam (our executive administrative assistant) who upon hearing what happened brought me a nice large Starbucks coffee and sweet treat.

I was grateful for the interactions with Alessio and all that he had taught me.

I was grateful for Sherri who put up with my antics on a daily basis.

In a sick way, I was grateful for missing my family because those feelings of pain, frustration and longing, made me realize what was most important.

During those tough days, I was grateful for moments of peace and quiet, silly jokes with friends, and the wrestling podcast I listened to on the way in to work every day.

There was so much to be grateful for, and when I shifted my thinking, I grew a little less stressed and a lot happier. At the very least, I could muddle through the day with some enjoyment. At the very best, I was able to focus on all the great things that were still around me. I did not journal at this point, but I did take a few moments every day before going to bed to reflect on two or three things I was grateful for. It started to work.

The science behind gratitude shows that not only does it build resilience, but those who are mindful and practice gratitude are happier and show decreased levels of stress. Dr. Robert Emmons is a professor of psychology at the University of California – Davis (UC-Davis) and has done extensive research in the area of gratitude. He states:

> *"The practice of gratitude can have dramatic and lasting effects in a person's life. It can lower blood pressure, improve immune function and facilitate more efficient sleep. Gratitude reduces lifetime risk for depression, anxiety and substance abuse disorders, and is a key resiliency factor in the prevention of suicide."*

According to Emmons, practicing gratitude no only makes you happier, but increases vibrancy and makes you more empathetic. A guy like me can definitely use more empathy in his life because so much of my thinking has its foundation in career driven success. Taking the time to give thanks can sometimes help me to see a situation from another's point of view.

For example, I remember clashing with a coworker on an implementation strategy for a software we had just purchased. We had strong opposing views, and one day we were hashing out our differences. I decided to listen for once, and for that I was truly grateful – especially when I did my evening reflection. As she spoke to me, I began to understand the different pressures she was under, and the forces that were influencing her decision-making. She was under pressure to deliver not just on that software package, but two other software implementations that had nothing to do with me. Having been in a similar position at a different institution, I felt for her. I still did not agree with anything she said, but I was able to calm myself and temper my temper.

Being habitually grateful only happens when you practice it daily. Ironically, I became the very person I mocked in college by keeping a gratitude journal. To steal and adapt a bit from legendary comedian Chris Rock: there is no point in hating anyone or anything. Don't like gratitude journals? You'll be writing every day. Hate Canadians? Your daughter's coming home with the owner of a Tim Horton's.

Since we're talking about Canadians, there is a three-piece process to building your GQ (gratitude quotient). As we say in my native Canada, GQ is a product of the excessive *EH's*. Do Canadians really say this? In my Canada, we do.

Emotion: Gratitude is a largely emotional undertaking. It requires you to clear the noise in your head and feel. If you are like me, this can be difficult at first because you are either uncomfortable visiting those feelings, or are so busy and consumed with career you forget that they exist. Once you are comfortable in that space you can be brave, and share that emotion with someone. That can be terrifying, but also largely gratifying when you see how people react to you. I connected with my fifth grade teacher just to tell her she was awesome. I was terrified to reach out because I could be totally ignored or laughed at (not a likely outcome but you never know, right?). Tapping into emotion does not make you a weepy mess, it just means you are aware and totally honest with who you are and what you are feeling. When we are in touch with our emotions from a gratitude perspective, then we are aware and appreciative of all the great things that exist in our lives.

Habit: To build your GQ, then you have to make gratitude a habit. It doesn't take long. A few minutes a day to write and/or reflect on the positive is all that you have to do to entrench it into your life. Thank the universe daily and watch yourself progress.

For me it wasn't easy, but I worked at my increasing my GQ, and found myself making significant progress one year later.

EPILOGUE: aka SUPERHERO

It has been just over one year since Alessio challenged my work-life assumptions. In that time, I took deliberate steps to improve my situation and move towards a job and lifestyle that was more life giving. The process took much longer than I anticipated. I invested the time into interviewing many professionals both in education and in speaking to better gauge what the best fit for me was. I made significant progress on my PhD, and now see the daylight in terms of getting my degree. I had interviewed for jobs around the country, and hadn't yet found a great fit. I approached interviews as a chance to meet people and enjoy new locations in addition to applying for a job. I wanted the experience to be life giving and they were . . . even if I didn't get the job. I enjoyed great locales like Newport News, VA, Albany, NY and Chicago, IL.

I was in our basement with a now fully mature three-year-old Alessio when the phone rang. I did not recognize the number so I let it go to voicemail. Alessio and I were beginning to play superhero and villain. He was getting into Transformers, Spiderman and He-Man and I loved it. Playtime was now taking me back to my childhood in a completely new way.

Sorry phone, I have to keep Spiderman from thwarting my plan for world domination. You can wait.

We kept playing, but after twenty minutes curiosity got the best of me and I checked my phone. The voicemail icon lit up my screen as I logged in. I hit play and listened. It was a college I had interviewed with saying they wanted to do a reference check with my current supervisor. Earlier in the process the interviewers had told me that current supervisors were only contacted if a job offer was going to be made. Happiness was on the horizon. I went back to battling Spiderman.

One week later, I had negotiated my job offer and had given Shelly my two weeks' notice. In negotiating my final offer, I asked more questions about work-life balance, job expectations, and opportunities for growth than I did about compensation and benefits. This new position leveraged my speaking and leadership training skills. The job would also give me time more free time outside of work to funnel into my speaking business and more importantly, my family. Moments after sending my acceptance letter a memory of Alessio popped into my head.

I remembered how two weeks earlier my son and I had gone to the playground by our house. In addition to his Paw Patrol t-shirt and shorts, Alessio was wearing a red cape and a matching eye mask (like Robin) and had transformed himself into Super Alessio! He asked me to chase him around the playground and I obliged. As I was chasing after him he taunted:

"I'm too fast. You'll never catch me! I will win!" over and over again.

I watched (more like chased) in amazement. A year ago he just mastered walking, and the year before that he could barely take a few steps without stumbling. Alessio's first steps (like most babies) were awkward and shaky. At one point, he reverted back to crawling because it was quicker. Eventually his legs strengthened, walking became easier, and he quickly grasped it. Now he was running and mocking me all while adopting a super confident alter ego to boot.

Our work-life journey is a lot like a child learning to walk. The first steps are difficult, and often we revert back to what is comfortable and easier for us. Taking those first steps is scary, but if we want to strengthen our work-life legs, then we need to get up and keep making the attempt until we master it. No matter how many times a child falls, they all get up and keep attempting to walk. No matter how many mistakes we make or scenarios we are in that may not be work-life friendly, we have to keep moving forward and learning. It is a process that we grow from and become more comfortable with. People always ask me if I talk about work-life issues with my potential employers and I always answer yes without hesitation. It wasn't always like that and the first time I asked a work-life question to a potential employer I thought they would end the interview right then and there. They didn't, and it became easier each time.

My son wasn't pretending to be Super Alessio . . . he IS Super Alessio. As we strengthen our work-life muscles we uncover the confident superhero within us. The superhero who rescues us from our old unsatisfying life into one that is filled with purpose gives life to us and others around us. It mocks and challenges the old patterns that held us back. It shouts the battle cry "I'm too fast. You'll never catch me. I will win." over and over again. It may seem difficult to get to there, but if you're committed to a better life it becomes quite easy. So easy that even a two year old can do it.

THE 2-YEAR OLD'S
ACTIVITY BOOK

USING THE ACTIVITY BOOK

As I stated at the beginning of this book, some of you may wish to dive deeper into each of these lessons. This section contains various activities, reflections, and random acts of fun to help sharpen your work-life skills.

You may wish to write in this book and that's ok. Heck, I've left a few pages blank just so you can doodle and scribble.

If you don't like to write in book's that ok. A fillable .pdf version of these activities by going to:

www.paulartale.com/2yearoldsguide

CHAPTER 1 ACTIVITIES

Let's begin by reflecting on the following three questions. You may choose to write your response or you can simply think about them.

1) Why do I currently do what I do (professionally and personally)?
2) Is there harmony between work and life (and why or why not)?
3) What are the things that are keeping me from living the life I want (and why)?

Tying all of chapter one together. In the spaces below write down your why, your ideal job and then compare the elements between your current situation and desired situation.

Finding Your Why Worksheet

1) What's your why?

_____

_____

2) What is your ideal job?

_____

_____

3) List the key elements/benefits/features of your desired job?

- Element 1:

_____

_____

- Element 2:

  _____

  _____

- Element 3:

  _____

  _____

- Element 4:

  _____

  _____

- Element 5:

  _____

  _____

- Element 6:

  _____

  _____

4) Next, compare and contrast the key elements in your current job situation with your desired situation.

KEY ELEMENT	IS THIS PRESENT IN YOUR CURRENT SITUATION (YES/NO)

5) Add up the number of "yes" responses and the number of "no" responses and record it in the box below.

"Yes" responses =	
"No" responses =	

6) Answer this simple question: how far off is your current situation from your desired situation?

7) Reflect on this question: what is causing the imbalance between your current situation and your desired situation? How much of a change in your life will need to occur for you to make this happen?

8) List three action steps you will take to move towards a more why-centered life. The initial steps do not have to be monumental, but they do have to be specific with deadlines to keep you on track.

ACTION STEP 1:

_____

_____

DUE DATE:

_____

_____

ACTION STEP 2:

_____

_____

DUE DATE:

_____

_____

NOTES: List any additional information you may need
to complete this step.

ACTION STEP 3:

_____

_____

DUE DATE:

_____

_____

NOTES: List any additional information you may need
to complete this step.

CHAPTER 2 ACTIVITIES

ACTIVITY 2.1 SATISFACTION ASSESSMENT

Here I have provided for you a job satisfaction assessment for you to complete:

	Strongly Disagree	Disagree	Neutral	Agree	Strongly Agree
My job is important to the company I work for	1	2	3	4	5
The company mission and values fit my own	1	2	3	4	5
I find the work that I do to be fulfilling	1	2	3	4	5
I feel respected by my coworkers/peers	1	2	3	4	5
I feel respected by my supervisor	1	2	3	4	5
I would like to retire at this company	1	2	3	4	5
My job is a source of great pride	1	2	3	4	5
My job allows me to grow professionally	1	2	3	4	5
I would do this type of work for less money because I love it so much	1	2	3	4	5
Overall, my job positively impacts my personal life	1	2	3	4	5
I feel successful in my job	1	2	3	4	5
My company recognizes me when I accomplish something	1	2	3	4	5

I constantly think about working for another company	1	2	3	4	5
I feel certain that this is the right career field for me	1	2	3	4	5
I am doing work I am passionate about	1	2	3	4	5

Scoring the assessment. You should note that this assessment acts as a simple gauge for your satisfaction. To get your score, simply add up all the numbers you have circled. The lower your score the more dissatisfied you are. Conversely, the higher the score the more satisfied you are. Scores in the middle range indicate there are some elements of your current work situation you find fulfilling and others that are not. If this is the case pay attention to the questions that scored high and low. See if you can find patterns.

ACTIVITY 2.2: IDENTIFYING LIFE-GIVING

Answer this one this one simple question for every major activity or job you participate in:

NAME OF JOB/ACTIVITY:

_____

_____

This job/activity I currently do excites me and makes me a better person? True   False

NAME OF JOB/ACTIVITY:

_____

_____

This job/activity I currently do excites me and makes me a better person? True   False

NAME OF JOB/ACTIVITY:

_____

_____

This job/activity I currently do excites me and makes me a better person?   True   False

ACTIVITY 2.3: THE TWO-MINUTE DRILL

If you are still having trouble determining what exactly is life giving try this activity.

Step 1: Grab a stopwatch or use the app on your phone

Step 2: For one-minute write down all the activities/jobs/tasks that you currently engage in that excite you, energize you, and give you life. Write continuously. Don't think – just write down what comes into your mind. Trust your natural instincts.

Step 3: For one-minute write down all the activities/jobs/tasks that you WANT to engage in that excite you, energize you and give you life.

Step 4: Look at your two lists and decide if you need to group your answers into categories. You may find much of what you wrote down may revolve around topics like health and fitness or consulting others. See if you can find common categories.

Step 5: Circle the one category (or it could be a singular task) that you feel gets you excited and adds to your life.

Step 6: Answer these questions below. There are two sets of similar questions. The first set addresses whether you want to turn your life-giving category into a career, the second addresses it as a hobby:

Career Focus

1) Can what I selected turn into a career?
   YES   NO
2) Can what I selected be turned into a career right now?   YES   NO
3) Do I want that career to be full-time?
   YES   NO
4) Do I have the knowledge to turn this into a career/money producing part time business?

   YES   NO

5) What do I need to learn to move this toward becoming a career or business?   List three questions you want answered so that you can move forward.

   Question 1:

   Question 2:

   Question 3:

6) List three resources you will engage with that will help you better understand how to turn your life-

giving category into a career. Resources can be books, seminars, interviews with successful people in the field, conferences, websites, etc. Be specific in your answer. For example, do not just say "website." List the actual website.

Resource 1:

Resource 2:

Resource 3:

Hobby Focus

1) Am I currently engaged with this topic as a hobby?
YES   NO

(If you answered NO to #1) What do I need to engage with this as a hobby? What are some organizations, conferences, etc. that I need to connect with to ensure this life-giving hobby is in my life?

ORGANIZATION/RESOURCE 1:

ORGANIZATION/RESOURCE 2:

ORGANIZATION RESOURCE 3:

2) Would I like to devote more time to this hobby?

YES   NO

(If you answered YES to #2) How can I make more time for this hobby? What current practices am I engaging in that are not life giving, or can be cut to make room for this hobby?

ACTIVITY 2.4: RESILIENCE NOW

Hall of Fame.   Fill in the chart below and start inducting moments into your Hall of Fame. Start by filling out one example in the chart. You can add more below afterwards. The chart below exists to help you catalogue events. Your real Hall of Fame list can be much simpler. I have included a "speaking hall of fame" list that I personally keep as an example.

REALM OF SUCCESS	INDUSTRY OR FIELD	EXAMPLE
Award		
Degree or Certification		
Personal Achievement		

PAUL'S SPEAKING HALL OF FAME LIST

1. Playing Football at the University of Toronto (if I can achieve that I can achieve anything)
2. Top 30 out of over 35,000 contestants at the 2018 World Championship of Public Speaking
3. Qualified Member of National Speakers Association
4. 12 public speaking trophies and awards
5. Pechakacha and Ignite Presentations
6. Distinguished Toastmaster Designation
7. Repeat Clients
8. Hundreds of Rave Reviews (so many I don't know what to do with them)
9. Defensive Line Coach at the NAIA All-Star Game
10. Being recognized on the street by people who have seen my presentations (I am like a K-List celebrity).

ACTIVITY 2.5: *CELEBRATE SMALL VICTORIES*

Please list below three small victories that you can use to motivate you when times are touch.

Example

EXAMPLE SMALL VICTORY: Two quarterback sacks during training camp.

EXAMPE LESSON(S): (optional): 1) Small victories matter. 2) Evidence that I can perform at a high level can be found. 3) I am resilient enough to get through anything.

SMALL VICTORY #1:_____

LESSON(S): (optional):_____

SMALL VICTORY #2:_____

LESSON(S): (optional):_____

_____

_____

SMALL VICTORY #3:_____

LESSON(S): (optional):_____

_____

_____

ACTIVITY 2.6: JOIN THE JEDI

In the space below, list your current mentors and possible mentors for you in your life. Follow the example.

CURRENT MENTORS (GOAL)	POSSIBLE MENTORS (GOAL)
Joe S (*Work-life research*)	Ed J (*Keynote Speaking Business*)

Follow up question: For those who are possible mentors, answer these three questions for each person:

1) Have I met person yet?
2) Have I asked them to mentor me or to give me advice? (If no, answer HOW you will reach out to them)

3) How will I utilize this person's wisdom?
4) How often do I want to be in contact with them?

ACTIVITY 2.7: EMBRACE THE PROCESS

At some point in our lives we have all followed this process. I know that as a parent I do this because I have no other choice. I try something out with my son and if it does not go as planned, I think on it, try something different and apply it again. Think of a time in your life when you have applied the process. Fill in the boxes below.

EXPERIENCE	
WHAT DID YOU LEARN FROM IT?	
WHAT DID YOU LEARN FROM REFLECTING AND/OR GETTING FEEDBACK?	
WHAT CHANGES DID YOU MAKE FOR THE NEXT TIME AROUND?	
HOW DID THE NEW EXPERIENCE GO WHEN YOU MADE THE CHANGES?	

CHAPTER 3 ACTIVITIES

ACTIVITY 3.1. THINK ABOUT IT.

Think critically about those whom you really love spending time with and those who bring you down. No need to write anything. Just think.

ACTIVITY 3.2. BEAR OR YAK?

In the chart below, provide at least one tactic that will allow you to spend more time with them (if they are a positive influence) or less time with them (if they are a negative influence). In the case of the latter, determine if cutting those forces out of your life is possible, and, if so, take steps to do so.

BEAR/YAK ROSTER AND STRATEGY CHART

NAME OF PERSON	BEAR OR YAK (AND WHAT TYPE)?	WHAT WILL YOU DO TO INCREASE OR DECREASE THE TIME YOU SPEND WTH THIS PERSON?

BEAR/YAK ROSTER AND STRATEGY CHART

NAME OF PERSON	BEAR OR YAK (AND WHAT TYPE)?	WHAT WILL YOU DO TO INCREASE OR DECREASE THE TIME YOU SPEND WTH THIS PERSON?

CHAPTER 4 ACTIVITIES

ACTIVITY 4.1: NO! I SHOULD BE...

What should you be saying *no* to in your life? Fill out the statements below for three situations that resonate with you. Not all situations need to be work based.

I should be saying NO to_____

_____

Instead I should be (enter action item) _____

_____

I should be saying NO to_____

_____

Instead I should be (enter action item) _____

_____

ACTIVITY 4.2: MORE QUESTIONS TO PONDER

1) Think of a time your boundaries were crossed. What was the situation? How did you handle it? What could you have done better?
2) Does your current job fit your work-life boundary style? Please describe.
3) What role do phones and technology currently have in your work-life situation? Do they detract or add to your life?
4) How does your current job compare to your dream job/lifestyle when it comes to work and life? What are the significant differences (if any)? How does technology factor into both your present and desired situation?

ACTIVITY 4.3: TALK TO YOUR BOSS
Set a meeting with your supervisor to discuss your work-life situation and preferences. If you have regular meetings, this can be built into your agenda as an action item. This may seem scary, but it is a necessary step in improving and/or maintaining your work-life situation.

ACTIVITY 4.4: A VIEW FROM THE TOP

Interview people. Find two or three people who are successful in your field. Reach out and interview them about what work and life looks like from their perspective. Write down the key lessons you learned from the interviews.

CHAPTER 5 ACTIVITIES

ACTIVITY 1: LET'S PLAY WIH LEGO!

This activity has four very simple steps.

1) Put three minutes on your stopwatch, and make a list of all the activities that incorporate play that appeal to you.
2) Rank your activities from the most desirable to the least, and transfer them to the left column on Chart 5.1.
3) Next to each activity, determine if it is something you want to do daily (D), weekly (W), monthly (M), or annually (A). Mark the designation in column two.
4) Write out how much time you think the activity will take of your time in column three.

Chart 5.1: Playtime! Example.

ACTIVITY	(D)aily/(W)eekly/ (M)onthly/(A)nnually	Time Needed
Comic Book Convention	A	48 hours (2 days)
Brain Games App	D	15 minutes
Karate Class	W	3 hours
Family Vacation	A	1 Week
Catch up with Cousin Sal (my best bud)	W	45 minutes

Now You Try!

ACTVITY	(D)aily/(W)eekly/ (M)onthly/(A)nnually	Time Needed

At this point, you may be asking what do you do once you have ranked and analyzed time commitments for activity #1. You might be saying, "that's nice Paul, but what do I do with this? I am short on time as it is." If that's the case, then let's move on to Activity #2.

ACTIVITY 5.2: ANALYZE YOUR TIME

To the best of your ability, I want you to think about how your average week breaks down. Fill out another worksheet below. This one will ask you to list a daily function, estimate how much time you spend on it, and to convert that time into a percentage of your week. If you spend less than one hour on a task then just convert it to a fraction. For example 15 minutes =0.25, 20 30 minutes = 0.5, 45 minutes = 0.75 and so on. Tasks are everything you do. Sleeping, eating, commuting, grooming, working (obviously), watching shows, surfing the internet, taking care of children, exercising, etc.

To find out your percentage, simply take the amount of time you spent and divide it by 168 (the number of hours in a week). For example, if I spent 10 hours per week commuting to and from work, I would do 10/168 = 0.059. So I spend 5.9% of my week (or 6% if I want to round up) commuting to work.

BONUS: There is also a weekly time analysis spreadsheet located in the electronic activity book package. Visit www.paulartale.com/2yearoldsguide to access it.

ACTIVITY	TIME SPENT	% OF WEEK
Sleep	56 hours	33.3%
Watching Netflix	16 hours	9.5%
Commuting to Work	5 hours	3%

ACTIVITY 5.2: ANALYZE YOUR TIME (continued...)

Your Turn:

ACTIVITY	TIME SPENT	% OF WEEK

Looking at how your time is spent, reflect on the following questions:

1) Where do you spend most of your time (top 3)?
2) What are some areas you are spending too little time on?
3) Is time for play/recreation even on your list? Do you feel it is adequately represented?
4) Where are do the most inefficient uses of your time occur?
   a. Based on your selections, what inefficiencies can you cut down on to make time for play?

b. Write down your new time chart below. This chart will help you track your proposed versus actual time spent on task. Commit to playtime for the next four weeks or until you feel play is better incorporated into your weekly structure.

ACTIVITY	TIME SPENT (PROPOSED)	TIME SPENT (ACTUAL)

*A note on activities you may have marked as annual. Something you do once a year (or just once like skydiving) is something that can't be accounted for using the forms above. That being said, make sure you complete the following action steps to make sure these important annual play dates are maintained. I have included some blank spaces for you to insert more specific tasks as needed.

Annual Playdate Checklist

[ ] Vacation time booked from job (if needed)
[ ]   I have determined how I want work and my vacation to interact during this time.
[ ] Funds set aside to make playdate happen – if none then check the box below.
[ ] Savings plan created to save for annual playdate.
[ ] Reservations for playdate have been made (hotel, travel, reserving my spot etc.)
[ ] _____

[ ] _____

[ ] _____

*Make time to incorporate play into your life daily. If you can, find other people to join in on the fun!

THE ONE SIMPLE CHAPTER 6 ACTIVITY

ACTIVITY 6.1: JOURNALING YOUR PAST

Take a few moments and ask yourself "what happened?" Journal what circumstances got you to this point of work-life imbalance. Be honest with yourself. Don't think of solutions. Just seek to understand the conditions that have taken you to where you are now.

CHAPTER 7 ACTIVITIES

ACTIVITY 7.1: ANALYZE THIS....

Let's take some time to analyze your situation using the Six Questions. You will want to get a pad of paper/word documents out to really work on this OR you can download the fillable .pdf from www.paulartale.com/2yearoldsguide

Situation:_____

1) What can't I control?

2) What can I control?

3) What has actually changed?

    1) Has there been announcement of change? If yes, then:
        a. Does the announcement impact me directly?
            [ ] YES [ ] NO
        b. Does the announcement impact my supervisor directly?
            [ ] YES [ ] NO
        c. Has the announcement given complete information?
            [ ] YES [ ] NO
        d. Is the change immediate?

[ ] YES [ ] NO

e. *Am I excited about this change?*
[ ] YES [ ] NO
f. *Can I live with this change?*
[ ] YES [ ] NO
g. *Does this change impact me negatively?*
[ ] YES [ ] NO
h. *Is this change a deal breaker where I will look for work elsewhere?*
[ ] YES [ ] NO

5) What course of action will I take right now?

a. *Would it be helpful to gain further clarification from someone?*
b. *Do I need to get ahead of this change and reach out to other individuals/departments?*
c. *Can I get by just doing my job as it was before the change?*
d. *Is there information/data I need to gather and have ready for when the change comes?*
e. *Do I require counseling to cope with the change?*
f. *Do I need some extra training that will make me competent or useful during the change?*
g. *Do I need to investigate other career/job options?*

6) If events aren't to my liking, what is my exit strategy?

If you are considering an exit strategy, remember the six steps:

- *Are your materials in order?* Do you have an updated:
  a. CV/Resume
  b. Cover letter template
- *Define your destiny. What do you want?*
Answer this question: The job I am looking for is _____ (job title/job type) with a minimum salary of _____. I am willing to relocate (or commute) within _____ miles of where I currently am.

- *Reach out to your network*
  a. *List five contacts who can be of immediate assistance for advice, guidance, or leads. Make a plan to contact them within twenty-four hours.*
- *Build your network. There are two elements to look at here:*
  a. *What associations, groups, or events can you attend to reach out to people?*
  b. *Do a social media analysis. How many connections/followers do you have on social media outlets?*
- *Get your finances in order.*
- *Friends with feedback. Create your feedback database. See example sheets below.*

CHAPTER 8 ACTIVITIES

ACTIVITY 8.1: WHAT'S YOUR WORK APPLE?

Answer this question: What's your work apple? In other words, identify one area that you are choosing short-term gratification over long-term growth.

ACTIVITY 8.2: SEVEN TYPES OF WELLNESS

FIRST→ Go Back to the Seven Types of Wellness. Write a score from 1 to 5 (1 = extremely poor, 5 = extremely well) on how well you think you are doing regarding this type of wellness in your life.

TYPE OF WELLNESS	SCORE (1-5)
Social Wellness	
Physical Wellness	
Spiritual Wellness	
Financial Wellness	
Emotional Wellness	
Social Wellness	
Environmental Wellness	

NEXT→ Identify one of the Seven Types of Wellness that you just scored that that you feel needs immediate attention and using the three E's, fill out the form below:

Type of Wellness Identified:_____

Educate: What do you need to learn and where will you learn it?

Experiment: Write down the ninety-day action plan based off your research.

Evaluate: Put your results here.

CHAPTER 9 ACTIVITIES

For this section, you can choose one or both of these exercises. They are simple, straightforward and essential for building gratitude in your life. To do these exercises, find a quiet space in your house. Remove all distractions and set a timer for three minutes. Just three. That's it. Complete these tasks daily.

ACTIVITY 9.1: THREE-MINUE REFLECTION

Three-minute reflection. Take three deep cleansing breaths, and reflect on all the things you have to be grateful for that day.

ACTIVITY 9.2: THE GRATITUDE JOURNAL

Gratitude journal. Get a book (or an app for the tech lovers) and for three minutes each night write out all that you are grateful for that day.

BONUS: At the start of every week, write down three to five words that describe how you are feeling. As an alternative, you can start the week by writing a few sentences about what your challenges, hopes, and fears are, and how you will try to deal with them. In both cases, see if the habit of gratitude changes your perceptions over time.

*Use the space on the next page to write down your three-minute reflection or to begin your gratitude journal (or both!)

EPILOGUE ACTIVITIES
(aka tying it together)

The previous activities were designed to get you to think and plan. They were deeper dives into each of the nine lessons that Alessio taught me.

With that in mind, I know that change can be overwhelming. Achieving what we call work-life balance does not happen overnight. It is a series of baby steps that you take. Just like a baby those first few steps can be wobbly but with time they stabilize and you begin to walk with confidence. Before you know it, you are running around as your parents rearrange the house to accommodate your new abilities.

It is time to take those initial steps. Below, simply list the ONE step you are going to take in each of the nine areas. One action for each. That's it. Here we go.

1) What's your why (in 10 words or less)

2) What makes you SO HAPPY?

3) List one Yak you are going to distance yourself from. List one Bear you are going to spend more time with.

4) What is the one thing/behavior/situation you are going to say NO! to in order to move forward.

5) Name the one playful activity you are going to incorporate into your life?

6) What is one positive healthy behavior you are going to start (Diet, exercise, counseling, meditation, a weekend in Vegas etc.).

7) What are you most grateful for?

8) Do you understand what has led to your current work-life situation? If No.....go back to to Chapter 6. If YES then ask yourself Question 9:

9) Is a change in career or work situation appropriate? If NO then GREAT! If YES then it's time to make a move. If you are a considering a career/job change then visit:

www.paulartale.com/2yearoldsguide to set up a free 15 minute career strategy session.

ABOUT THE AUTHOR

Paul Artale is a motivational speaker and author who speaks to organizations and people who want to perform at their peak. As a career coach Paul helps people find the harmony between their work and profession. Paul is also a PhD candidate who researches work-life flexibility and the impact it has on workplace performance. Paul has written and presented on the subject of work-life balance for several national publications.

Paul's "Why" in life is to spread his message and to help others find perfect fit between what they love and what they do.

For more information visit:
www.paulartale.com

Book Paul to Speak
(No pun Intended)

I would love to speak to your group and spread my message of overcoming challenges and designing lives that have meaning. In short, here are my signature programs:

The 2-Year-Old's Guide to Work-Life Balance. Really? Do you want me to explain it? Aside from what you just read, this workshop can also help companies be more work-life friendly in their design.

Hit Hard: 3 Must-Have Mindsets to (re)Design Your Life. Learn the three key principles to creating a life that is fun and fulfilling by hearing about how I overcame physical disability to achieve my dream of playing college football.

Unleash Your Message: Unlocking the Story that Inspires. As an award winning public speaker, I will share with you the tips, tricks, and drills necessary to deliver outstanding presentations. You have a phenomenal story inside you. I will help you unlock and unleash it on the world.

Contact Paul

www.paulartale.com

913-749-2489

paul@unleashyourmessage.net

@PaulArtale

linkedin.com/user/paulartale